MORE THAN A MECHANIC

PLAYING TO YOUR STRENGTHS FOR SUCCESS

GAIL T. BEBEE

Foreword by Deborah L. McFadden

Published by CRE Companies LLC / Cesar R. Espino

More Than a Mechanic / Gail T. Bebee - 1ST Ed

ISBN: 978-1-960665-34-8 (eBook)
ISBN: 978-1-960665-32-4 (PaperBack) Black and White Edition
ISBN: 978-1-960665-33-1 (HardCover) Black and White Edition
ISBN: 978-1-960665-35-5 (PaperBack) Color Edition
ISBN: 978-1-960665-36-2 (HardCover) Color Edition

Disclaimer

Some names and identifying details have been changed to respect and protect the privacy of individuals. I have tried to recreate events, locales, and conversations from my memories of them. To maintain their anonymity, I may also have changed some identifying characteristics, such as physical properties, occupations, locations, and places of residence. Having said that, nothing has changed about the spirit and intent of the stories these generous individuals shared with me.

Dedication

To Bruce Bebee, the love of my life. You are the man of my dreams and prayers.

To the memory of Mitzi Bebee, Bruce's first wife. Though we never met, I feel a deep connection.

To our four children: Donna, Tom, Bruce Jr., and Patricia. Know that you are loved unconditionally, always and forever.

To our eight grandchildren, eight great-grandchildren, and those to follow: May you thoroughly enjoy hearing these family stories and remember them as you shape your own destiny with joy in knowing that you are made to shine in your own unique way.

To the would-be entrepreneur: May you find your path to success and enjoy life.

Epigraph

It has been said that we discover our life's purpose when we identify our unique strengths and begin to use them. We discover our life's meaning when we use those strengths for the sake of others.

~ Larry Coulter

Table of Contents

Foreword

Having served as the former U.S. Commissioner of Disabilities, being one of the authors of the Americans with Disabilities Act (ADA), along with being a mother to children with disabilities; two of whom are elite Paralympic athletes and having experienced disability personally, I have dedicated my personal and professional life to fostering equal access and opportunities for the growth and personal success of individuals with disabilities.

In the pages ahead, you will find the extraordinary life story of Bruce Harper Bebee—a narrative that weaves together the enduring power of family, the joy of meaningful work, and the conviction that no challenge, not even a disability, can define a person's potential.

This book is, above all, a celebration of family. From Bruce's earliest days in Ohio, through the adventures and trials that shaped his journey, it is clear that the love and support of family have been his anchor. The stories of laughter, resilience, and togetherness are not just anecdotes; they are the foundation upon which Bruce built his life and legacy. The warmth that radiates from these pages is a testament to the bonds that have sustained him through every season.

Bruce's passion for business is equally inspiring. His curiosity and ingenuity led him to create solutions that changed industries, and his entrepreneurial spirit was always fueled by a desire to serve others and to innovate. He built not just companies, but communities, places where employees became friends, and friends became family. His story is proof that when you pursue your work with heart and integrity, success follows.

Perhaps the most powerful message in these pages is that disability does not define a person. Bruce's early struggles with reading and writing could have limited his future, but he refused to let them. Instead, he leaned into his strengths, worked harder than anyone, and ultimately became a voracious reader later in life. His journey is a beacon of hope for anyone who has ever felt held back by circumstance or limitation. It is a reminder that our true measure is found not in what we lack, but in what we choose to develop and share with the world.

I have had the privilege of knowing Bruce, his wife Gail (the author), and his family personally since 1983. I have witnessed firsthand the authenticity and generosity that fill these pages. Whether Bruce was solving a mechanical problem or sharing a laugh over a family meal, his humility and kindness were unmistakable. The stories you will read here are not embellished; they are the lived reality of a man who built his legacy on love, hard work, and an unwavering belief in others.

As you read, may you be inspired by Bruce's journey—by the love of family, the joy of meaningful work, and the courage to rise above adversity. Let this story encourage you to believe in yourself, nurture your relationships, and remember that every challenge can be transformed into a legacy.

Sincerely,

Deborah L. McFadden

See What Others Are Saying About Bruce Bebee

"Bruce transformed purpose into meaning. He gave himself away for the good of others."

~Larry Coulter

"Bruce always treated people fairly and was not afraid to give people second chances…"

~Brad Campbell

"His life is a powerful reminder that success is built on belief, hard work, integrity, and a lifelong commitment to growth."

~Max M

Acknowledgment

To all who contributed to this book—our family, friends, and colleagues—thank you for trusting me with your stories. You have touched our lives in many ways. I am deeply grateful for your contributions and for your willingness to share your lives with us.

To my brother, Curt: Thank you for your support and for your thoughtful feedback as I finalized the manuscript. I never knew you were such a fine editor.

To my sister, Karalyn: Thank you for your timely sleuthing skills and for encouraging me to say “yes” to happiness.

To Felisha: Thank you for showing me that writing a book is possible.

And to my husband, Bruce Harper Bebee: Thank you for your stories, your dedication to living a healthy and productive life, and for sharing your life with me. I love you with all my heart.

Preface

Maybe you've picked up this book because you are an entrepreneur, wanting to glean from a story of success.

Or

Perhaps you are frustrated with a circumstance or disability that complicates your desired path.

Or

Maybe you are in the film or broadcasting industry and are curious about the man behind the equipment you've come to love.

Or

Maybe you are a family member who wants to know more about your roots and the guy you know as "Dad," "Papa," or "Grandpa."

I wrote this book for all of you.

Overnight success is never "Overnight". Where we are today is the result of all the decisions, circumstances, more decisions, attitudes, and next steps that have finally brought us here. Bruce Harper Bebee is no different, except that he continually plays to his strengths and doesn't let circumstances paralyze him. He has stories… oh, so many humorous, adventurous, daring, life-threatening, pragmatic, compassionate, and even loving stories. It's a story for anyone and everyone who seeks inspiration, a good laugh, a fond memory, gratitude, or hope.

Over the last seventeen years, I've experienced the laughter and surprise of our friends whenever one of Bruce's stories came up. One of his employees even told him that if he ever wrote his autobiography, no one would ever believe it. His life stories are a culmination of several life choices that landed him right in the middle of major historical events. It's a history of respect, perseverance, brilliance, love, risk, adventure, service, generosity, growth, prayer, grieving, healing, and yes, overcoming challenges. It was through a recent series of personal growth seminars we attended together that I finally committed to putting this life story into print.

To recount these stories in his own words, I clipped a recording device to his shirt while we were driving across the western United States to visit family for the holidays. Family members, friends, and colleagues gave me more stories, photographs, memories, and a lot of patience as I wove them all together, often burning the midnight oil in each RV park or home we visited. What a journey! It was a fantastic, heartwarming experience together as we traveled the road, my laptop clicking away, actually on my lap.

Whatever it is you seek in your own life's destiny, may your journey be blessed as you create your own amazing story.

Introduction

Bruce Harper Bebee was solving complex mechanical problems long before he could enjoy reading a book. Life handed him real challenges, including an inability to read or write beyond a third-grade level well into adulthood. No one gets a pass. We all have our challenges, whether they are physical, emotional, financial, or family-related; this list can be endless. When it comes to creating success in your life, it's best to play to your strengths rather than paralyze yourself by focusing on obstacles. That is the story of entrepreneur mechanic Bruce H. Bebee. Bruce always knew he was smart. In fact, he was an expert at "fast math" and could engineer complex mechanical solutions in his head. He has been fondly referred to as "The Forrest Gump of Mechanics." Why? Bruce's life unfolds across decades of history, weaving tales of adventure, innovation, courageous risk-taking, and love. He played to his strengths, had confidence in his abilities, and addressed the inconvenience of reading challenges through hard work, persistence, and determination, allowing him to surpass his peers in a high-stakes military technical school—even earning the honor of Airman of the Month and becoming a Missile Launch Crew instructor.

Bruce built two successful businesses, earned his pilot license in ten days, returned four months later, earned his Instrument, Multi, and Commercial ratings in just three weeks, and continues to run a business at age eighty-three. Business highlights range from the White House to the Grand Canyon, from Thailand to remote Alaska, from Hollywood blockbuster films to an extra in cowboy scenes, from the 1984 Olympics to high school football, from community service events to the Secret Service, from the Rose Parade to lifeguard competitions, and from search & rescue to NASA Space Shuttle landings. His stories highlight technical ingenuity, operational reliability under pressure, and a willingness to work in challenging environments worldwide, underpinning a reputation as a go-to provider for complex broadcast and film power/lighting needs. He's fit at eighty-three, still doing pull-ups and dips, lifting weights, running three offices, traveling the world for fun, and encouraging young people to "Do something you love." That's good advice, and it continues to serve him well.

CHAPTER ONE

Simple Beginnings

Believe in Yourself

You don't choose where you begin your life, and that's no accident. In fact, wherever you get your start is the perfect place for you to build the foundation upon which you will grow. Bruce is the fourth of six siblings. Born in Cleveland, Ohio, in 1943, he was a total surprise to his mother twenty minutes after the birth of his twin sister, Vicki. Bruce insists he was being a gentleman by letting ladies go first when exiting the womb. Vicki insists that he was just too scared and that she needed to make sure it was safe enough for Bruce to venture out. The twins spent a lot of time together while growing up and, to this day, have such a wonderful way of interacting with each other.

Because Bruce's father, Clinton (Clint) Bebee, worked in the critical steel industry supporting the war effort, he was deferred from the military draft during World War II. He was apparently a very strong young man and loved telling his kids about how the men spent their time during lunch breaks at the steel mill.

Apparently, the guys challenged one another to see who could achieve the most repetitions of overhead presses with a 150-pound well stone (used back in the day to cap abandoned water wells). According to Clinton, he was the reigning champion. Now, since this book is published as a historical fact, it must be true.

Bebee Siblings, New Athens, Ohio, 1952
Back Row: Vicki, Gary, Margo, Bruce H. Bebee
Front Row: Brent, Brian

It was the middle of World War II. Just after the birth of their twins, Bruce's parents, Clint and Lillian Bebee, moved the family from Cleveland to the small farming and coal-mining town of New Athens, Ohio, in the spring of 1943. There, two more siblings were eventually born to the family, completing their family of eight (two adults, six children). Early childhood in the Bebee household brings back memories of an outhouse in the backyard (yes, that means taking care of business outside or in a pot on the porch), a well with hand pumps in the backyard and kitchen, a Victory (vegetable) Garden, and chickens. They enjoyed riding their pet Shetland pony, and maybe a few slides on cardboard down the stairs.

Bruce's father, Clinton, wore many hats in New Athens. He was the company draftsman and photographer for Hanna Coal Company, Boy Scout Leader, Justice of the Peace, a 32nd Degree Mason, Sunday School Superintendent, Volunteer Fireman, and was as strong as anyone. He was very mechanical and passed that down to his boys, teaching them to use tools. When they started driving, he taught the boys how to repair their cars. Says Bruce's older brother Gary, "Our father was methodical, precise, and slow, producing everything with precision. He always worked, with his highest priority being to take care of the family. He was an all-around good man. He passed down a good moral compass to us all."

Lillian, Bruce's mother, was an intelligent and beautiful woman of strength. In her younger years, she was a Christian Evangelist, speaking in front of large groups. She was always active in the church and was a member of the Order of the Eastern Star. As was common during World Wars I and II, she had a "Victory Garden" that provided food for the family. She was an excellent gardener, canning the family harvest of fruits and vegetables every year. Bruce recalls fresh apple and rhubarb pies, as well as many summer meals consisting simply of bacon cooked with green beans picked fresh from their Ohio garden. Lillian sewed wonderful clothing for the family and was a great cook.

The Bebee siblings attended Franklin School for K-12 students in New Athens, which originally operated as Franklin College from 1818 to 1919, educating prominent graduates such as two governors, eight U.S. senators, nine U.S. Congressmen, and twenty state legislators, as well as John Armor Bingham. Bingham, inspired by the life of his classmate Titus Basfield (a formerly enslaved person), became the primary author of the 14th Amendment to the U.S. Constitution.

Eventually, the campus became the Museum of New Athens in the early 1990s and houses many photos stamped and dated on the back, “Photo by Clint Bebee”, Bruce’s father. This same museum also displays drawings and a photo of a pumper truck Clint designed and helped build for the New Athens volunteer fire station. The rich history of the Franklin property makes for a wonderful showcase of early memories from the Bebee family.

Circa 1950 Fire Pumper Truck Designed by Clint Bebee, New Athens, Ohio. Clint Bebee (Bruce’s Father) on the far left.

Life as a young child in New Athens was simple. They played outside, learned about nature, and Bruce joined the Cub Scouts. Bruce and his siblings looked forward to the annual Fireman’s Carnival and canvassing the town with pillowcases to collect candy on Halloween. There were frequent family gatherings: visits to see Aunt Vi and Uncle Burgess near Steubenville; Grandma Flossie and Grandpa Mac in Wheeling, West Virginia; Uncle Douglas and Aunt Mary Katherine in St. Clairsville; and Lillians dad, Grandpa Dick (known as GPD), a former police officer in the

1920s followed by a railroad career but most remembered in the family for having had 18 wives (not all at the same time, of course). It was a small-town life in the Midwest, filled with neighbors who all knew each other. Seventy years later, New Athens townspeople still recall the Bebee kids.

Cub Scout Bruce H. Bebee (middle) and Boy Scout Gary Bebee (far right), New Athens, Ohio, 1950

As the mother of two girls in the family, Lillian was determined that Bruce's sisters, Margo and Vicki, would not marry a coal miner. It was a tough life she did not intend for her daughters. Hence, in the summer of 1953, she convinced Clinton to give up his many community roles and move the family to Southern California. They packed up the family, including Grandma Flossie, in the family '49 Pontiac Woody station wagon. Bruce was ten years old at the time and remembers the station wagon towing an overloaded homebuilt trailer.

Somewhere in Jerome, Arizona, the engine

overheated and died as they tried to climb a steep hill. Suddenly, the station wagon started rolling backwards, so the entire family bailed out, leaving Clinton to maneuver the vehicle as it rolled back downhill into a safety railing at the edge of the slope where it finally came to a rest. With all family members accounted for, they eventually jumped back into the vehicle and went on their merry way. There were sketchy hotels along the way and a top-secret swimming pool incident in Las Vegas, but there are some things better left untold. To this day, Bruce and his brothers are extremely grateful to their mother for insisting on the move out west, as they all achieved success in their chosen paths.

Clinton worked the rest of his career, starting as a machinist and as a quality control inspector at Douglas Aircraft, later to become McDonald Douglas Aircraft. Lillian took an adult school class on soldering and worked on the production line at Hughes Aircraft for several years. She actually offered to teach Bruce how to solder! The family of eight resided in a two-bedroom, one-bath house in Lawndale. They were so grateful their new home had indoor plumbing! Life was exciting with this new convenience. Bruce recalls that the only privacy was in their one bathroom, with the door shut, and that there was typically a line of family members waiting in the hallway for their turn. They all got along and functioned this way without difficulty. As recently noted by Bruce's brother, Gary, this may be why their current homes all have multiple bathrooms. The four oldest children, Margo, Gary, Vicki, and Bruce, shared a bedroom, while Brent and Brian roomed with the parents.

It was a childhood full of the Southern California experience: riding bicycles to the beach, pulling off water-balloon attacks on unsuspecting passersby, and all that comes with six young siblings growing up in a place where kids rode bikes until dark. I've heard stories of swinging from ceiling lights and crash landings, but somehow, Clinton and Lillian managed to keep six kids corralled well enough.

Well, except for the plunger story in which the ever-so-innocent Vicki and Bruce were doing dishes. This was in the days before garbage disposals, so kitchen plungers came in handy to unclog the sink. Somehow, the kitchen plunger magically made its way up to the ceiling to see if it could make itself stick. Always so helpful, Vicki and Bruce climbed onto the stove to see if they could remove the plunger from the ceiling. It seemed to them that the best way to remove it was to hold on to it and jump, letting gravity do its job. Instead of the plunger letting go, it held on to the ceiling and pulled a nice round piece of plaster down, leaving a hole in the ceiling. When mother Lillian arrived home, she wondered what happened to the ceiling. The kids, of course, claimed, "We don't know. We were just doing the dishes and the ceiling fell (in a perfectly round shape)." To which Lillian calmly replied, "Well, it's an old house. Things are bound to happen." Says brother Brent, "You know, they believed that story for a very long time."

At age fourteen, Bruce began his first job as a newspaper delivery boy for the Los Angeles Examiner (founded by William Randolf Hearst in 1903). Brother Gary recalls, "All of us kids were employed from our early teens. It was part of the Bebee family life. That is, having pride in taking care of ourselves instead of relying on government or anyone else to do it for us." Bruce and Gary began every day by waking at 3:30 am, bicycling to the office by 4 am to fold newspapers, then loading them to head out on their routes. They each had their own route of 150 customers, six days per week, and 200 customers on Sundays. They would make it back home with just enough time to have breakfast and get to school. Twin sister Vicki recalls at least a few early mornings in which she rode on the back of the bike and tossed the papers while Bruce zipped along the streets of Lawndale, California.

Roughly a year into their newspaper delivery career, the two brothers were running into a few challenges. They had customers who tried to beat them out of the $1.50-per-month subscription, which came directly out of the delivery boys' pockets. The newspaper company always got paid. That's when the two entrepreneurial brothers decided to up their strategy and increase their income by becoming newspaper subscription solicitors in addition to their delivery job. Bruce (age 15), brother Gary, and three other friends earned the title of the championship solicitation team. For their accomplishment, they won an all-expenses-paid trip together to Yosemite.

Bruce and his siblings attended Leuzinger High School in Lawndale, California. According to brother Gary, Bruce was always likable and made friends easily. He was (and still is) a math wizard, working calculations all in his head and having no idea how to show his work on paper. He achieved high marks in three classes: math, shop, and tennis. As for the rest, it was a struggle. Bruce could barely read at a third-grade level. He recalls not being able to distinguish the difference between "was" and "saw" even into his adult years. Whether it was a lack of phonics instruction or a form of dyslexia, we will never know. When there was a written test in any class, Bruce could not decipher the instructions and would simply sign his name at the top of the page, turn it in to the teacher, and leave class. This typically earned him a C or D in the class and was enough to graduate from high school. Extracurricular activities included four years playing singles on the varsity tennis team, a year in a church youth group, and working as a box boy at Arico's Market.

According to Bruce's younger brother, Brent, Bruce was rarely home during his high school years. He was either playing tennis or working. Arico's closed at 10 pm, so Bruce frequently came home around 10:30, about the same time his mother returned from work. They would often share a freshly made beef chili tamale, laden with onions, from the hamburger joint on the southwest corner of Hawthorne and Rosecrans Ave. Bruce worked roughly 30 hours per week as a box boy from the age of fifteen until graduating high school in 1961 and enlisting in the United States Air Force (USAF) in February 1962.

One of Bruce's high school friends referred to Bruce as a late bloomer. His lack of reading and writing skills did not define who he was. He played to his strengths: mechanical ability, athleticism, and work ethic. As a retired teacher, sister-in-law Toni Bebee underscores this point, "Mechanical and artistic skills are intelligences that need to be respected. These strengths are valuable, and they've been under-celebrated." She is absolutely correct!

Now octogenarians, a group of Leuzinger High School classmates still gather for lunches, reunions, and reminiscing. Within this group are many accomplished classmates, including an FBI agent, an author, police officers, business owners, and all-around good people. Ronnie Barnes is one of those friends. He recalls, "During the middle to late 1970s, I ran into Bruce at the Hilton Hotel and Casino in Reno, Nevada. He said he was just taking a relaxing minute after a long week of negotiations and meetings. As usual for him, he looked all relaxed and smiling. As we caught up on our lives, he said he was there with the Hilton group and had to call it a night and get some sleep. They were going out on a hunting trip early the next morning. From my time in the police department, I knew about Barron Hilton. He was a no-nonsense kind of guy who surrounded himself with other very successful people. Bruce did not brag about it. He was just excited to go hunting."

CHAPTER TWO

Creating a Unique Set of Skills

Bruce H. Bebee, Lackland Air Force Base, USAF Basic Training, 1962

Every step you take has the potential to prepare you for your next breakthrough, achievement, or calling. Bruce developed a strong work ethic at his grocery store job, and after high school, he was offered the opportunity to become a cashier with benefits. However, he knew that wasn't for him and enlisted in the United States Air Force at the age of eighteen. This was the Vietnam draft era. Bruce evaluated his options between the Air Force and the Navy because both offered technical training. Since he couldn't swim, he figured joining the Navy was out. He began this journey as all airmen did, with five weeks of boot camp in San Antonio's Lackland Air Force Base. From there, he attended Power Generation School at Sheppard Air Force Base in Wichita Falls. This assignment played to his mechanical skills, and his future was now in motion.

Once assigned to his duty station at Elmendorf Air Force Base in Anchorage, Alaska, he found himself traveling to remote early warning military sites throughout Alaska, including the Aleutian Islands. He performed maintenance and overhaul on diesel generators throughout the region, often navigating freezing temperatures to 60 degrees below zero. This California boy recalls walking an eighth of a mile from his barracks to the chow hall, and then another eighth of a mile (outside of course) to the power generation plant house, where he would find himself hugging a diesel engine to get warm. I don't know if maybe this is where he acquired his respect for the power of engines, but it certainly set him up for his next steps.

Bruce was clearly good at what he did, earning the title of "Airman of the Month" for Elmendorf Air Force Base in Anchorage, Alaska, his second year on base. He was called in for an interview for Airman of the Year, during which he realized that his lack of reading had left him behind on current events, and he was disqualified.

One of the most memorable moments during his time in Alaska occurred on Good Friday at 5:36 pm, March 27, 1964, when Bruce was in his barracks. He thought the world was coming to an end. It was the largest earthquake on record in the United States and North American history. It felt so severe that the only thing he envisioned was an old comic book in which the world was coming to an end, with people floating off. Bruce and his roommate hit the floor and hung onto the bedframe for dear life. They were experiencing the infamous 9.2-magnitude Alaska earthquake, which lasted nearly three minutes. Some portions of Alaska were permanently raised by as much as thirty feet, while others dropped by up to eight feet. There were landslides, tsunamis, fires, and general mayhem, even hundreds of miles away. Five people were killed in Anchorage during this quake. One of these was a friend who was instantly killed when part of the JC Penney building fell and tragically crushed him on the sidewalk. Bruce recalls his car jumping from one lane to the other and back again as he was driving during one of several aftershocks exceeding 6.2 in the weeks following the initial quake.

Bruce's next and final Air Force assignment landed him at Vandenberg Air Force Base, California, where he was hand-picked for the Strategic Air Command (SAC) Atlas F Missile School in August 1964. The Atlas F Missile System had a nuclear warhead to be used in the event of an attack from other countries with nuclear weapons. Each evening after school, there was a reading assignment that his peers could typically complete in less than an hour. However, with Bruce's reading challenges, it would take him hours. He overcame the challenge by using a dictionary to help him decipher unfamiliar words one at a time. He was determined and persevered, oftentimes for long hours, while his buddies stayed out partying. Perseverance once again paid off! He completed SAC Missile School at the Top of his Class, even surpassing officers who were college graduates. And, wait for it.... They made him a Missile Launch Crew instructor because he understood the material so well. Hard work and dedication, playing to your strengths, pay off. With this, you can overcome just about anything!

Bruce and his fellow crew members were considered the elite of the SAC missile group. As a member of the missile launch crew, Bruce wore pressed white coveralls, a starched round cap, and spit-shined shoes. Each crew member worked roughly 80 hours per week on a rotating schedule of 24 hours on, 24 hours off, 24 hours on, and 48 hours off, with one-hour briefings before and after each shift. They worked inside the 180-foot-deep missile silos that housed the missile and all its mechanical instrumentation. The control rooms, sleeping quarters, and a kitchen were off to one side, and the missile was on the other. To enter, they would go down one level underground to the entrapment doors. The outer door had to be closed before the inner door was opened by someone already on the inside. They would relieve the prior five-man crew and remain for the next 24 hours, performing maintenance, studying, and practicing drills. Out of 24 hours, they were allowed to sleep for six.

There was a red phone with two keys at his station that, if called upon, meant that his crew would be responsible for pushing the button to launch a nuclear warhead missile at enemy targets. Fortunately, that phone never rang. Bruce and his squad were awarded Launch Crew of the Month and Launch Crew of the Year in 1965. In December, the warhead was replaced with a satellite. Bruce's crew topped off the year by launching that satellite from Vandenberg AFB (Air Force Base) in December 1965. To his knowledge, that was the end of the Atlas F missile silo program. The Atlas F silos were decommissioned and replaced by Minuteman silos.

Strategic Air Command Atlas F Missile Launch Crew of the Year. Bruce H. Bebee on the far right.
Photo taken at Vandenberg Air Force Base, 1965

Bruce left the United States Air Force after four years of military service. He was living in Santa Maria, California, and took a job with Union Oil as a roustabout in March 1966. Duties included digging foundations for oil dikes, driving big trucks, and loading salt into steamers that brought oil to the surface of the sand reservoir so it could be pumped.

A couple of months later, in June of 1966, Bruce was interviewed and hired for his technical and mechanical strengths at the Philco Corporation. Within a month, they sent him overseas to Thailand. In this capacity, Bruce was a civilian contractor working on US military contracts for power generation services supporting US Army communications between Thailand and Vietnam during the Vietnam War. For reference, Philco was a Ford Motor Company subsidiary that was formally renamed Philco-Ford Corporation in 1966. Bruce's time there was filled with adventure, crazy stories, and a stubborn supervisor.

In his new position, Bruce's mechanical skills were quickly noticed by his superiors. He came up with a simple fix for major power outages affecting multiple generators across multiple sites. He was sent all over the region to provide this fix, saving Philco the contract. Following this, one of his responsibilities was to request parts when the machinery needed maintenance, but the supervisor kept denying his requests. This led to additional power failures, which his supervisor blamed on Bruce for lack of maintenance. Heads were going to roll! Thankfully, Bruce had the opportunity to demonstrate that his supervisor had denied his parts requests. Realizing Bruce would never get a fair shake from his supervisor, the regional manager offered Bruce the option of choosing any site he wanted to work at next.

Bruce transferred to another section of Philco-Ford that operated hard fixed communications sites. There, his responsibilities included troubleshooting and repairing generators throughout Thailand. Twenty-four-year-old Bruce and his coworker were given a company car with a chauffeur to troubleshoot and repair generators across the region for nine months. His assignments took him to Korat (also known as Nakhon Ratchasima, a major city in northeastern Thailand), Phitsanulok (a historic city in lower northern Thailand on the Nan River), and Bangkok (Thailand's capital in the central plains). It was quite a life!

At times during this assignment, Bruce lived in an American-style, two-story house with a concrete floor, built directly adjacent to a swamp/rice paddy in the city of Korat. Thankfully, he lived to tell many a story about snakes, spiders, and more snakes. It was a Saturday at 8 am, so he was not working that day. Because of the heat and lack of air conditioning, they relied on big floor fans, open windows, and open doors for circulation. Bruce noticed a green snake in the room. He recognized it as one of a few "three-steppers" in the region. This means that it was highly venomous, and within three steps of its bite, you would cease to live. Lovely!

The snake was coiled around the base pole of the big floor fan. Bruce instantly grabbed the first thing he found, a military-grade bug killer, and started spraying the snake. This only caused the snake to come at him. Bruce retreated to the kitchen and hastily climbed onto a chair as the snake followed. A few days earlier, Bruce had purchased a lovely 3x4-foot felt painting, as was popular at the time. From his perch on the chair, Bruce looked down and noticed a seven-inch-diameter spider emerging from behind the frame. The spider was on its way to attack the snake when Bruce diverted the bug spray from the snake to the spider. The spider ran back behind the velvet painting. Bruce quickly kicked the frame, thus crushing the giant spider. And the snake? Well, Bruce momentarily lost sight of it until he noticed it was now climbing up his chair! Jumping onto the kitchen table, Bruce sprayed more bug killer and vigorously bounced the chair. Finally, the snake lost its grip and eventually fell to the floor. As the snake was swinging its head back and forth, ready to strike, Bruce lined the chair leg up and crushed its head in one blow. You never know when athletic ability will come in handy. Fortunately for Bruce, that was the end of the snake. He decided it was time to go for a walk and left the crushed snake on the floor for the housekeeper.

Bruce seemed to attract the local "wildlife." During his assignment at a military facility in the Province of Phitsanulok, Bruce worked with a military partner who had a military jeep. To get back to their base for lunch, they would typically take a shortcut across a field, following a worn path straight through six-foot-high Thai grass. It was ¼ mile instead of taking the longer ¾-mile road. As they headed across the field, they saw what they thought was a ten to twelve-inch diameter “log” across the path. Confident in his driving skills and the jeep, the driver decided to run it over. As the front wheels hit, a large python snake raised its head from the tall grass, roughly seven feet above ground. It gazed straight at the two men in the jeep. Apparently, it didn’t like being run over like a log! The driver didn’t stick around to find out what the snake was going to do about it, so he hit the gas and high-tailed it out of the field. The snake incident was reported, and the next day, a grader was sent out to clear the field. Roughly two-thirds of the field was graded when the snake rose over the front of the blade. The operator jumped out, and the grader ran over the snake, killing it. The dead snake measured between 21 and 24 feet long, and thankfully, everyone lived to tell about it.

And again, in Phitsanulok: same driver, same jeep. Having previously learned his lesson about taking shortcuts through the field, this time the military driver took the ¾-mile-long dirt road to lunch on base. Halfway through, Bruce and the driver saw a four-foot-long snake slithering across the road. The driver ran over it and confidently slammed on the brakes to slide and kill it. Having passed the location by more than 20 feet, the two men got out to see if the snake was dead, but couldn’t find it. Giving up, they walked back to the jeep, only to see the snake sitting on the floor of the driver’s side of their vehicle. Needless to say, the snake was known to be very venomous, so the two men decided to leave it alone, abandon the jeep, and walk back to base.

Armed with broad experience working in power generation at both temporary and fixed communication sites, Bruce was eventually tasked by Philco-Ford to assess all sites in the region to evaluate contract staff, make 100 staffing cuts, and recommend improvements for each site. Guess who was at the top of the cut list? The supervisor who denied ordering necessary parts, of course! Guess who was at the bottom of the list? Bruce added his own name, as he was ready to head back home to the United States.

It was the end of summer in 1968 when Bruce flew back to the United States via military transport amid the era of Vietnam War protests. Bruce, a civilian, disembarked the plane to be greeted by protesters throwing insults at him and his military counterparts. "Baby Killers," they shouted! It was a rude welcome home after serving with such skill and integrity. It was truly one of those historic and emotionally difficult times in American history

CHAPTER THREE

Back Home

"Hey Beautiful"

Some meetings are brief enough to be dismissed—until they quietly change everything. Returning from Thailand to Southern California late in the summer of 1968, Bruce met Mitzi during a chance encounter in the South Bay region of Los Angeles County. Bruce and a friend were walking into the Rain Tree, a popular dancing and nightclub in Torrance, when he couldn't help but notice a beautiful young lady leaving from the same door with her friend. Bruce recalls the moment, "Mitzi was petite and literally beautiful," so that's just what he said. His first words to Mitzi were, "Hello, beautiful, where are you going?" She responded, "We're leaving." Not one to be pushy, Bruce simply acknowledged, "Okay, goodbye." The girls walked outside while the two guys continued inside. The moment seemed lost forever.

Less than a minute inside the nightclub, Bruce remembers feeling a presence behind him. It was Mitzi. She announced, "We decided to stay." This single decision changed both their lives. Bruce recalls them spending the evening getting to know one another, finding out that she had two children and that she was widowed roughly a year prior. The young couple enjoyed a powerful connection, but Mitzi and her two children were leaving the state early the following morning. They were moving back to Massachusetts, to be with her family. Their magical evening seemed destined to be just a memory. However, undeterred and planting a seed of hope for a future reunion, Bruce gave her his phone number and said, "If you ever come back to California, call me." And that's just what she did.

By January 1969, Mitzi was back in town and working as an Executive Secretary at Northrop Aircraft. Bruce's long shot paid off. The two spent quite a bit of time together, along with Mitzi's children, Donna (age 5) and Tommy (age 4). Bruce recalls young Tommy asking him if he would be his father and marry his mother. Shortly after Tommy's innocent request that they become family, the two adults were sitting in the car when Mitzi asked Bruce why he had never married. Bruce responded, "I've never met anyone that I felt was capable of taking care of my family and me if something ever happened to me." Mitzi quietly took that in. The next day, she turned the tables on tradition and put herself on the line, "I was thinking about what you said. Would you marry me?" To which Bruce immediately responded, "Yes." He saw her not just as a beautiful woman, but as an equal, a "good match" with profound capability and independence. Bruce admits, "I know that sounds unusual, but it's still how I feel today. Besides, with Tommy and Mitzi both asking me, how could I possibly say no?"

The couple was married in September 1969. Their relationship was a fusion of deep affection and practical synergy, built on mutual respect for each other's distinct strengths. To this day, Bruce's description of Mitzi is deeply admiring, warm, and respectful. He describes her as "literally beautiful" and embodying everything he "always wanted in a woman."

Bruce and Mitzi Bebee Wedding, September 1969

From the time he met Mitzi until they married, Bruce tried out different jobs. This became most helpful in identifying which careers he did not want to pursue. At Mattel Toys, he was the only person to ever ace their mechanical skills test. He was accused of cheating until he baffled the interviewer by answering oral test questions. He worked there for a couple of months. Thinking he might follow in his brother Gary's footsteps as a police officer, he briefly attended the LAPD Academy but realized that was not the life for him either.

Bruce finally landed a position more suited to his skill set at American Mark (now defunct), a small company with government contracts to test and qualify 5k and 7k generator sets.

In 1971, Mitzi gave birth to their second son. Bruce felt an increasing sense of responsibility and pride, naming their new son Bruce T. Bebee (Junior). Mitzi was able to take maternity leave from work, but there was a definite lack of sleep as she and Bruce took turns getting up in the middle of the night. It was perfect. The whole family was excited to have a baby in the house.

After waiting to ensure that Junior and Mitzi were healthy and stable, Bruce attended Northrop Tech (1972-1973) to acquire his Airframe and Power Plant Mechanics (A&P) license. While he never worked as an airline mechanic, he gained multiple skills, including welding, electrical, hydraulics, pneumatics, dope & fab (fiberglass), and more. Bruce recalls this training as key in rounding out new skill sets and refining the skills he already had, making him confident he could accomplish whatever he set his mind to.

The young couple purchased their first home in Torrance, California, in 1973 while Bruce was finishing up his sixteen-month program at Northrop. This purchase, three years after they were married, cemented their shared values of stability, security, and independence through property ownership. It established a foundational belief that they continued to value for years to come.

Upon graduation from Northrop Tech, Bruce was offered a job at a major airline, but he was not interested. Even before graduating, he was offered a position at F&B/CECO, a nonunion rental company for the motion picture industry. "The way the employment ad read, it involved traveling, driving mobile equipment trucks, and operating generators. It just seemed like it was a perfect job created for me." This proved to be a pivotal moment in defining a career set in the motion picture industry. Bruce was responsible for all the gear, such as cameras, generators, lighting, and grip equipment, in a production unit. It was 14 to 16 hours a day on payroll, and another three hours setting up and charging all the batteries, then putting them back on the truck, ready for the next day. It was a long, hard, low-paying job, with a few fun experiences working on film locations for "Death Wish" with Charles Bronson, "Terminal Island", and the famous Evel Knievel jump over the Snake River.

Movie equipment in 1973 was expensive, such as the high-speed, soundproof camera that Bruce's supervisor tasked him with "clean up and repair anything you feel is necessary, and replace any bearings that are making noise" before it went out on a job. Within four hours, Bruce had the entire camera disassembled into subsections and methodically laid out piece by piece (screws, bearings, gears, nuts, bolts). Imagine the supervisor returning at 5 pm to check progress, "Oh my God, Bruce, what did you do? I hope you can put that back together because nobody else here knows how!" To which Bruce, totally confident in his skills, replied, "If nobody touches this, I can have it back together tomorrow." They covered it and placed a padlock on the door so no one could get in. Bruce was instructed to be there at 7 am and, by lunchtime, had the camera fully back together. The praise came with conditions, "I've never heard a camera that quiet, and don't ever do that again!" Bruce can disassemble and put things back together in his head. He has tremendous confidence in himself. He knew how the camera worked, and he knew he could put it back together. It's a unique set of skills.

As a veteran, Bruce qualified for the GI Bill to

purchase property. Always mindful of opportunities to improve the family's financial security, he and Mitzi purchased a rental property in Torrance. The total cost to close on their first rental property was $900 on a zero-down loan. "The irony of that was Mitzi and I thought we got ripped off," he chuckled. Their first two properties laid the foundation for future business and investment decisions. Their interest was piqued, leading both to obtain their real estate licenses. Mitzi stayed active, working in real estate for about five years with Century 21.

Meanwhile, Bruce began working for Bob Teasley at American Mobile Power in 1974. This required Bruce to become a member of International Brotherhood of Electrical Workers (IBEW) Local 40 Hollywood Union. Bob was having two generators built and hired Bruce to operate them for the movie industry. Bruce's first job on location was "One Flew Over the Cuckoo's Nest," filmed at the Salem, Oregon Mental Institute for four months. Fun fact: if you look hard enough in the movie, you may catch a fleeting glimpse of Bruce as an "extra" on the stairs leading to the docks in Depot Bay. You may also catch a quick shot of "cowboy extra" Bruce in "Nickelodeon" (1976), a film directed by Peter Bogdanovich about early Hollywood. Other assignments included "Born Innocent" in Albuquerque, New Mexico, and then "Baby Blue Marine" in Shasta, California. After one of these trips and eleven months on the road during his first year with Teasley, Bruce's wife, Mitzi, met him at the airport and drove him straight to the attorney's office. "I didn't get married to be alone" was all she really needed to say to make her point that his extended work travel needed to end.

Cowboy Bruce H. Bebee, an "extra" in "Nickelodeon" 1976

Fortunately, Bruce had already started visualizing how he could make Bob's generators better by making them quieter. He approached Bob with his ideas and was told, "Leave my equipment as is, and when you build your own, you build them any way you want." That was the deciding moment for the direction of Bruce's future. He started mentally designing his concept of soundproof generators in 1974 and left the company roughly a month later.

Through his IBEW Local 40 Hollywood Union, Bruce was assigned a one-day job that turned into three years as the night-shift electrician at KTLA Studios on Sunset Boulevard in Hollywood. Thank you, John McQueen (KTLA shop foreman), for saving Bruce's marriage with this opportunity, since constant travel with the union was not conducive to a happy wife. Bruce worked at the studios from 1975 to 1978. This was the early beginnings of the Donnie and Marie show. Bruce enjoyed occasional conversations with them. He also enjoyed watching the two young musicians learn to ice skate at the KTLA rink built on stage specifically for their show's signature ice-skating segment, which was part of the show's identity.

The KTLA electrician's job involved multiple responsibilities, including stage maintenance, being available for maintenance calls, and making rounds for seven stages. This provided Bruce with some downtime when things were running smoothly and gave him the headspace to further develop his concept for portable soundproof generators. Using his experience, recognizing the needs of the film industry, and applying his experience with power generators, he worked to expand on his ideas. He wanted to mount his future equipment on a four-foot-high truck bed, so he imagined his early designs by moving tape around on a wall to determine the most convenient location and heights of controls for an equipment operator.

CHAPTER FOUR

Believe in Your Idea

Bebee Generators is Born

Behind the man with an idea was Mitzi Bebee, a woman of strength, faith, and belief that her husband could accomplish his goal of building a soundproof generator. Mitzi didn't want Bruce to have any regrets, so Bebee Generators was born in 1977. They sold their first home and rental property, downsized into a smaller home in Torrance, and used the gains to fund construction of the first two soundproof generator sets for the movie industry. Friend and colleague, Jay Crawford, recalls working on chalk layout designs on the pavement with Bruce while the kids ran in and out of the house. Beneath his backyard awning after hours from his work at KTLA, Bruce built his first two generators on a single truck: one with 120 volts DC and the second with an AC single- or three-phase output. Both were gas engine-powered.

ABC was the first client, using Bruce's new generator truck for five days at a theater in Santa

Monica. His second generator job was powering mobile video trucks at the 77th PGA Championship Golf Tournament at the Riviera Golf Club in Beverly Hills. This caught more attention because low-noise generators were not commercially available at that time. A visit to Paramount Studios' electrical department led to immediate interest in purchasing, which he declined. Bruce knew he had answered the call for a better product and aimed to build a rental fleet instead. Bruce and Mitzi reinvested the proceeds immediately into the construction of their second twin-generator truck. These two trucks provided the only studio sound quality AC generators in town. Bruce designed and built all units himself to meet strict noise, portability, and capacity requirements best suited for his customers.

Design breakthroughs that made Bebee Generators so desirable included aluminum housings lined with soundproofing material to reduce noise. Even today, generator construction still incorporates these soundproofing innovations. Additionally, he provided versatility for his clients by mounting both AC and DC units together on a truck, with 1800 feet of 4/0 cable on hydraulic reels. With the rapid success of Bebee Generators, Bruce kept building more sets in his backyard. He was granted flexible hours at KTLA to accommodate the generator business until he finally left KTLA in 1978. Says Bruce's brother Gary, "It took Bruce and Mitzi's courage and fortitude to move forward and eventually dominate the movie and generator industry."

With the rapid success of Bebee Generators, the need arose to move operations out of the backyard. They relocated their work to a shop on Del Amo Blvd in Torrance, just a half mile from their home. Within roughly a year, they outgrew that rental property and purchased a one-acre property on Figueroa Street in the city of Gardena, California. As the company expanded even further, Bruce and Mitzi purchased the adjacent one-acre property with another building in 1985, where Bebee Generators stayed for roughly five years. Mitzi provided administrative genius with fierce competence, while Bruce handled the shop, technical matters, and training the operators. The two complemented each other beautifully to form a solid business partnership, with Mitzi even asking Bruce to accompany her in taking an electricity course at El Camino College so she could gain a better understanding of the terminology required for improved client support.

Their success allowed the family to sell their house in Torrance and move to Huntington Beach. This is where they finished raising their three children, Donna, Tom, and Junior. Huntington Beach was a growing new community at the time. There were many families, great schools, and, of course, beach life for the kids.

The generator units were widely used in film, television, sports, and government applications. These projects ran the full spectrum from extremely high-profile, high-stakes contracts to those that were truly off the beaten path. The stories all play a part in history, from intense to simply just outright fun. The Village People recorded their famous 1980s music video aboard an aircraft carrier in San Diego using Bebee Generators. To this day, you may catch Bruce with a reminiscent smile and a little shimmy whenever he hears the song "YMCA," recalling his early entrepreneurial days.

April 14, 1981, marked the first Space Shuttle landing at Edwards Air Force Base. Mission SSTS-1 was the first landing of a reusable orbital spacecraft returning from space, proving that the shuttle system could launch, orbit, and return safely to Earth. Networks such as ABC, NBC, CBS, and multiple international outlets required power to cover the historic landing of Space Shuttle Columbia. Before the landing, Bruce was called to a NASA meeting of engineers and multiple media representatives. During the meeting, the ABC executive stood and requested, "We would like Mr. Bebee, who owns Bebee Generators, to establish a maximum noise level for all generators on-site." Bruce specified 60 dB at 10 feet, which the NASA engineers considered impressively quiet. Assuring NASA that his fleet was uniquely capable of meeting this standard at the required scale (about 14 generators), Bebee secured the exclusive contract for a six-day, 24-hour, multi-network power operation that allowed the world to witness space exploration history as it was made. Columbia promptly navigated into the hangar after landing, and a photo of Bebee Generators driving past the test Shuttle Enterprise was quickly taken to commemorate the event.

Bebee Generator truck with test Shuttle Enterprise, Edwards Air Force Base, 1981.

One of the more intense contracts was in 1983 when the U.S. invaded Grenada. The U.S. and other supporting Caribbean nations were there following a political coup that ousted the prior government. Bebee generators were flown in by military transport to provide power for White House communications and military housing while U.S. forces worked to restore order and protect American citizens there at the time, including numerous medical students.

From humble backyard beginnings, it was a time of rapid growth and recognition, including a prestigious White House Secret Service contract. From 1982 to 1988, Bebee Generators went wherever the President or Vice President went. Armed with Top Secret clearance from his Air Force years, Bruce trained President Ronald Reagan's Secret Service power generation teams to operate Bebee Generators worldwide, providing secure, isolated power for White House Communications. The generators were typically flown by cargo planes from a San Francisco-area base to meet these needs, including deployment to the G7 Summit in Venice, Italy (June, 1987), attended by President Ronald Reagan. The summit took place during Reagan's final year in office, amid easing Cold War tensions and ongoing economic challenges among industrialized nations. A Bebee 60 kW generator was mounted on a barge in a canal between the communications hotel and the Summit venue, as there was no land space for trucks. Similarly, any time Reagan visited his ranch, Bebee Generators supplied a soundproof generator dedicated to communications, again highlighting the need for quiet, reliable, mobile power in sensitive political settings.

Bebee Generators powering White House communications at the G7 Summit in Venice, Italy June, 1987

Mitzi functioned well as the CEO and Administrator of Bebee Generators. She enjoyed the office side of booking clients and getting to know them on a first-name basis. She had excellent recall as to their families, kids' names, and special events in their lives. With her at the desk and phones, Bruce was able to do what he loved in the shop and often on location.

There were times when Bruce could barely keep up with the rental demand at Bebee Generators. He had key team members who consistently showed up with a can-do attitude, allowing him to build the business. Eventually, this included Bruce and Mitzi's oldest son, Tom, who had just graduated from Marina High School. Tom brought in his friend, Steve Eakins, and the two young men began their adult careers at Bebee Generators. They handled deliveries, pickups, and operated generators, becoming versatile, go-to employees.

Tom's employment marked the start of hiring Bruce and Mitzi's children into the family business. Always curious as a young employee, he became an excellent generator operator and worked with his parents until they sold Bebee Generators. His friend Steve was full of energy. "I was working in the yard and told Steve I needed a particular wrench. He runs all the way into the shop to get the wrench and runs all the way back out. For Steve, there was no point wasting time walking." Steve is remembered as deeply respectful and sincere, always addressing Bruce as "Mr. Bebee" and using "yes sir, no sir." In gratitude, Bruce praises, "I would have loved to have had about 10 or 15 of him." I imagine it was both helpful and entertaining to experience the youthful energy brought to the company by Tom and Steve. Eventually, each young man started his own successful generator company. In addition to the obvious family and friend relationships involved, they've all maintained a business relationship with Bruce, with regular calls to discuss generators and the film industry.

In 1984, Bebee Generators became the sole provider of generators at the 1984 Los Angeles Olympic Games. They provided primary power for ABC's televised coverage at 23 sites and commercial power interfacing and transfer switches at eight additional sites. The design ensured seamless backup in the event of commercial power failure. Preparation for the fleet began six months in advance, including the construction of switchgear and the completion of new generators. Bruce recruited family and friends with mechanical/electrical aptitude as on-site operators. He recalls, "I literally had to bring in my brothers, my son Tom, my cousins, my friends, their friends, anybody who had the ability to understand what we were doing mechanically and with some electrical experience to operate because every generator had to have an operator with it." The final generator was finished only days into the Games after a 72-hour wiring marathon by

Bruce. To his great relief, the testing proved flawless, and it was immediately deployed. Bruce was given a free pass to attend any Olympic event he desired. Instead, he sent the final generator to its Olympic destination with an employee and sequestered himself for 2 days of sleep and recovery while everyone else enjoyed the events. He then emerged to make brief operational visits to the Olympic sites but did not focus on watching events. Such is the life of an entrepreneur who answers a challenge with resounding belief that it can be done. With the additional units for the Olympic Games, and Bruce only 41 years old, Bebee Generators *suddenly* became the largest generator business in the industry with 23 generator sets.

Mitzi and Bruce H. Bebee at Donna and Wally's wedding, Costa Mesa, California, 1988

By now, Mitzi and Bruce's daughter Donna was working with Bebee Generators. Donna, always capable, began working in the front office with Mitzi and then shifted to delivering and operating generators. Bruce recalls multiple requests from one of their customers, specifically requesting that Donna be sent on the job instead of the other operators. It took Mitzi's intuition and explanation for Bruce to grasp why this one company was so particular. Donna had met her future husband, Wally, on the job. The young couple married and eventually launched their own successful generator company.

Bruce provided mobile generators to power outdoor events for multiple Hilton Las Vegas events, which often included boxing. During these events, Bebee Generators provided power for the earth-based space satellite units, all the communications, venue lighting, and broadcast needs. Shortly before one of the fights, a short, athletic-looking guy named Mike started a conversation with Bruce at a café counter in the Hilton Hotel. It was only hours before the big 1986 Tyson/Trevor Berbick fight. You guessed it… it appears that Bruce had a lunch conversation with Mike Tyson on the day he became the youngest heavyweight champion in history at age 20 with a Total Knockout in the second round. For this fight, Bebee deployed 14 generators. Two 300 kW units were housed in 28-foot "dry van" trailers, one of which had an 8-foot-square carpeted control room with a drop ceiling, lighting, a recliner, a closet, and a TV, all built for comfort and for monitoring the on-board generator while on jobs. ABC production requested to seat Hollywood Rat Pack VIPs Dean Martin, Sammy Davis Jr., and Peter Lawford in Bebee's comfortable control room to watch the fight uninterrupted via the internal TV feed. After a brief introduction to the three icons, Bruce stayed outside on standby, explaining that if a power failure occurred, he would need immediate access to repair issues. Of course, nothing went wrong. Bruce designed his equipment with great attention to detail and logic, not just to ensure it was dependable and easy to service, but also to make it comfortable for even the most famous of celebrities.

ABC Sports utilized Bebee Generators for multiple sporting events, such as mountain climbing in Yosemite, Zion and Yellowstone, motocross, "Battle of the Network Stars" (celebrity athletic challenges), Super Bowl XXII (Jack Murphy Stadium in San Diego, 1988), Huntington Beach Surf competitions, and even famous stunts. Bebee Generators provided power for the media at multiple Robbie Knievel (Evel Knievel's son) stunts, including his 1989 jump over the fountains in front of Caesar's Palace in Las Vegas. Bebee powered large and diverse broadcast events where reliable, often redundant, power systems were critical for television coverage and venue operations.

Bruce and his wife, CEO Mitzi, were part of the first American film crew allowed in Moscow, Russia (October, 1988). For reference, 1989 marked the end of the Berlin Wall, which divided East Berlin (communist East Germany, backed by the Soviet Union) from West Berlin during the Cold War. Warner Brothers Television Studios contracted Bebee Generators to bring one generator to Russia for the TV sitcom "Head of the Class," which aired on ABC. Bruce and Mitzi traveled for a three-week job, but Bruce characterizes it as an experience he would not repeat. They stayed at the Rossiya Hotel, a 3,000-room property across from the Kremlin, then described as Europe's second-largest hotel. The rooms had concrete floors, and though the temperature was in the forties, the heat could not be turned on until November 1. They slept in long johns and wool socks. Guests were responsible for bringing their own sheets, towels, and toilet paper. Food access was challenging, as government-owned restaurants turned them away because they lacked reservations, even though there were no customers inside. Occasionally, a friendly hostess would seat them. Eventually, they found cafeterias on the hotel's floors, but Mitzi decided to leave after three days due to the conditions. One bright spot during this Russia experience included reconnecting with Mike Tyson, who had recently married actress Robin Givens. Robin played Darlene Merriman on the sitcom. Mike stayed at the American Embassy but would show up on location or at the Rossiya Hotel with Robin. Tyson told stories of joining Embassy noncommissioned officers for their mandatory two-hour daily workouts. He was friendly and well-liked. Navigating this trip gave Bruce an even deeper appreciation for freedom, capitalism, and the right to create your own destiny. Bruce suggests such an environment would make discontented Americans appreciate U.S. freedoms

"National Lampoon's Christmas Vacation" (the Chevy Chase holiday classic), filmed in Breckenridge, Colorado, provided Bruce with new design innovation opportunities. In 1989, he was called upon to deploy two sled-mounted generators onto winter ski slopes for mountain filming, where trucks could not drive. Despite providing production with detailed sled drawings and dimensions in advance, nothing was built when Bruce arrived on location. Using his welding skills, he and local help fabricated both sleds with integrated fuel tanks and generator mounts. The sleds were towable by snow tractors. He accomplished this within two days to keep the three-week shoot on schedule. This example underscores his hands-on engineering and problem-solving approach in remote, harsh conditions. One unit was placed mid-slope in a cut-out flat area. The second unit powered extensive tree lights simulating a town toward which Chase appears to be sledding out of control. Bruce remained onsite to ensure reliable operation, staying in a warming hut and checking the units every few hours.

As the company grew, Bruce was in the field less often. One day, Mitzi called him into the office. "I have a job you might want to do. Four days in San Bernardino. It's Mrs. Nude International at the park off the 15 freeway." Says Bruce, "It was one more adventure I could check off my bucket list." Bruce recalls their first contact at the nudist colony was a woman in her mid-70s, dressed only in a cap and tennis shoes. She was issuing parking passes and rules, explaining that crew participation in nudity was optional. Bruce found it more comfortable to wear his shorts and t-shirt; he also found it striking how people comfortably carried on with normal activities—conversations, sports, swimming, jogging—while nude, viewing it as simply a different lifestyle.

On the final celebration day, there was a western-style (2-story saloon, stores, hotel, etc.) façade and plateau where about 10 nude skydivers (men and women) were to land. They were wearing only harnesses, hats, goggles, gloves, and shoes. The first few came in pretty quickly, landing right down in the center circle in front of the facade. One of the later skydivers came in too low for the façades, so he started swinging back and forth, trying to get between the buildings. Unfortunately, he was a hundred and eighty degrees out because he impacted above a second-story window on the façade. The only thing spectators could see was him sliding down the second-story and first-story windows. Fortunately, he sustained only minor injuries. The last skydiver came in about five minutes after everyone else. He was new to the sport and coming in high, so he overshot the landing circle. He was in the process of trying to circle back to the landing spot, but was too low to make it past the adjacent rock slope. He landed in a 25-foot patch of cactus on the slope. Bruce recalls, "You could see the poor guy trying to swing clear of it, but unfortunately, he landed right in the middle of the patch, fracturing his ankle and suffering a massive blood blister where his heel hit his (behind), plus numerous cactus punctures covering one side of him from head to toe. He looked like he had the measles." Apparently, extracting the needles took about 30 minutes. Despite hearing of this horrible incident, Bruce's operators were eager to volunteer to provide generator service at numerous other nudist events in Palm Springs (a converted hotel) as well as Playboy Mansion parties hosted by Hugh Hefner in Beverly Hills.

CHAPTER FIVE

What "Retirement" Looks Like for a "Doer"

For someone like Bruce, "retirement" didn't mean slowing down—it simply meant building something new. By 1992, Bebee Generators had 52 soundproof units ranging from 60 to 800 kW, in trailers from two-axle towables to 40-foot units. Tired of the constant phone calls from film crews in the middle of the night, Bruce and Mitzi decided to sell to Young Generators, which General Electric eventually acquired. Friends and Family helped them celebrate with a big "retirement" party. However, their second company had already started in 1990 and had three lighting trucks by 1992. Since they were now operating only one company instead of two, this was a partial "retirement," and Bruce found himself with extra time on his hands.

Mitzi noticed that their kids frequently went to the Colorado River for fun with friends. This prompted Mitzi and Bruce to surprise them by purchasing an existing home on the River in Parker, Arizona. In true Bebee form, Bruce and his younger brother Brian (an accomplished contractor) constructed an 800-square-foot addition that included a new master bedroom, bathroom, and attached garage. They completed the remodel in six weeks.

Right after completing the river house remodel, Bruce earned a speeding ticket between Parker and Las Vegas, where he was to meet Mitzi. The speeding ticket was an inspiration to fulfill another dream. He earned his private pilot license by attending an accelerated ten-day program in San Diego and promptly purchased a high-performance single-engine Cessna.

After flying the single-engine for four months, Bruce decided it was too small (all entry and exit were through the pilot seat) and too slow (160 mph). He next purchased a 414 Twin-engine Cessna (230 mph) and almost immediately began a full-immersion, three-week accelerated proficiency program. This included flight school in Carlsbad, where he spent six hours a day flying and six hours a day studying. After this school, Bruce took his FAA exam flight and achieved Multi-engine, Instrument, and Commercial ratings. Twenty-two-year-old Mark Browne was his flight instructor and can verify that it was highly unusual to accomplish all this in just three weeks.

Bruce's airplane insurance required him to log 50 hours with an instructor, so he hired Mark to spend the next two weeks with him, marking a memorable "retirement" adventure. Bruce recalls those two weeks with a smile as they flew all over the western states to Hilton's ranch south of Tahoe, the river house in Parker, Las Vegas, Carlsbad, and Los Angeles.

Recalls Mark, "I got invited to play poker with the big boys at the Hilton Ranch, and I did not have the money to play. Bruce sponsored me, and the pots were not small. I was a little man at a big boys' table. Good times." And about the river house in Parker, "Bruce was so proud to show me the ramp he engineered and built to get the jet skis from the house to the water. Just amazing. He should have designed a plane as well as flown them."

The through-line of Bruce and Mitzi's shared life was a cycle of intense work punctuated by specific, activity-based getaways, frequently tied to their business connections. Even their trips to the river house exemplified a strong attachment to responsibility, a commitment to fixing and improving things, and a strong work ethic. Their personal getaway property in Parker often occupied much of Bruce's weekends with maintenance, making sure everything was in order before the next visit from the kids and grandkids. While Mitzi loved it as a place to relax along the Colorado River and visit the local Casino, Bruce loved having another reason to fly his plane.

Three generations of family, extended family, and friends enjoyed the river house and water sports for many years. Daughter Donna recalls that the river house became the meeting place for the entire family, including her brothers Tom and Junior and their families. Granddaughters Rebecca and Jenna recall going to the river house during their early childhood, just about every weekend their family could. They were riding on Sea-Doos with their parents, Donna and Wally, at a very young age. Grandsons Aaron, Kai, and Shea were there enjoying the river too. Son Tom enjoyed taking the nieces and nephews out on his boat. Granddaughters Rochelle and Brooke recall trips to the river house every summer to enjoy wakeboards, the boat, jet skis, and floats down the river.

In short, the river house provided exactly what was envisioned when it was purchased: a fun getaway with the kids and grandkids. For Bruce, it was all that and a project to work on. After all, he is a doer and always has been: passivity is not in his nature.

CHAPTER SIX

Believe That You Can Do It Again

It Wasn't a Fluke

After a successful run with Bebee Generators, Bruce felt the need to prove to himself and others that he could replicate that success, wondering if the first company was just a "fluke." This question lingered for over five years and was a primary motivator for his next venture.

The idea of a lighting truck first sparked while Bruce was providing generators for a Rose Bowl Football game. He observed a competitor's new mobile lighting truck, analyzed its design, and identified numerous drawbacks and inefficiencies. It prompted his initial idea of creating a very different approach. However, the true catalyst for starting Night Lights by Bebee (Night Lights) occurred later on during location work for a TV series set in the Pacific Palisades neighborhood of Los Angeles. Bruce and a producer watched a crew struggle for nearly two hours to position a scissors lift for lighting, only for it to fail because the ground wasn't level. The producer's comment, "there just has to be a better way," led Bruce to propose an all-in-one truck solution. The producer's enthusiastic "in a heartbeat" response confirmed the market need, and Bruce went home to start designing his first truck.

Bruce designed the Night Lights trucks as completely independent units, integrating the generator and lights on a single chassis. This design allowed for a rapid setup time of 7-10 minutes with a single operator. In contrast, his competitor's style truck had to tow its generator and light rack separately, requiring 1.5 to 3.5 hours and multiple people to set up. An additional contrast would be the time and labor costs of manual lighting setups: rigging scissors lifts with lights, cables, and a generator, which takes two to three men several hours every time the director wants a move. To provide such time and cost savings, Night Lights drivers must be highly specialized. They require a Class A license, mechanical aptitude, and common sense. Beyond driving (10-15% of the job), they are responsible for operating booms, generators, and lights, as well as troubleshooting and repairing. Their ability to set up, move, and re-light locations faster than film crews can prepare for the next shot provides immense value, saving production clients significant time and money.

Night Lights Truck 1 with three 12K HMI "big eyes", Gardena, California, 1990

Night Lights by Bebee started in 1990 with conventional 12K "big eye" studio lights, which Bruce progressively upgraded to 18K HMI and 20K incandescent fixtures. Bruce eventually switched to more powerful 6K HMI lights, mounting 15 on a single truck with a boom that could extend to 120 feet in the air. To ensure flicker-free lighting for film cameras operating at 24 frames per second (fps), each truck is equipped with generators using electronic governors for frequency stability. More importantly, the company uses electronic ballasts that convert 60-cycle AC power to DC and back to square wave AC power. This enables their lights to be used with high-speed cameras shooting up to 1,000 fps without flicker issues, a significant technical advantage. Each light is equipped with its own video camera and is linked to a monitor for positioning. The booms carrying the light rack can rotate 370 degrees. The light rack attached to the boom rotates 90 degrees right or left and tilts down 80 degrees. Each light rotates 270 degrees and tilts 180 degrees. In other words, each light can be controlled independently or together in any combination to aim them exactly where they are needed. His innovations quickly allowed Night Lights by Bebee to dominate the Los Angeles film market.

The company has extensive experience serving multiple industries with professional lighting. They routinely provide secondary lighting for commercials, news reports, movies, TV series, music videos, staging areas for The Pasadena Rose Parade, and sporting events. It's not unusual for truck placement to be as much as a quarter to half a mile away from the action. Whereas primary lighting is used for the first 10-30 feet of the set and the actors, secondary lighting, provided by Night Lights, illuminates a whole block, multiple blocks, or even the background scenery, such as mountains or trees. At sporting events, the trucks are often used to augment the existing lighting to increase the output needed for filming. Sometimes, the lights are actually used during the day to simulate the sun, allowing filming to continue all day with the "sun" remaining in a fixed position, possibly even through a window.

Night Lights by Bebee, the first three trucks, the third (middle) truck holding nine 4k HMIs
Disney Ranch, Los Angeles County, California, 1993

Night Lights by Bebee equipment is large, and they were running out of space on the two acres in Gardena. Finally, in 2002, Bruce and Mitzi purchased 2.7 acres on East Gladwick Street in Rancho Dominguez, where they built a beautiful 23,000-square-foot concrete tilt-up building envied by every firefighter ever assigned to conduct a safety inspection therein. It included roughly 6,000 square feet of office space, a kitchen, a master bedroom suite, additional bedrooms and showers for his drivers, and 17,000 square feet of shop space with 11 bay doors to accommodate up to 16 trucks. For a short while, it also included a greenhouse Bruce constructed out back to grow tomatoes, which his employees told him tasted great. He swore he never got one, so that was the end of his gardening attempts. In any case, the Gladwick property was the last piece Bruce and Mitzi acquired before Mitzi unfortunately passed away in 2009.

Night Lights by Bebee Fleet outside of the shop on E. Gladwick St., Rancho Dominguez, CA.
Photo Credit: Night Lights by Bebee, 2004

The list of films illuminated by Night Lights is long. Their niche is location work, not stage lighting. This requires mobile logistics, adaptation to varied environments (urban streets, deserts, airports, etc.), and coordination with production teams to light large exterior or non-studio interior spaces while meeting both aesthetic and technical constraints. Favorite movie productions that required overseas travel and creative access include "Jurassic Park" in both California and Hawaii, and four months on "Pirates of the Caribbean" (2003-2010) in the Bahamas, which involved complex beach shoots and a barge to light a ship at sea. Other movies include several of “The Fast and the Furious” (2003-2016), with one LA street-racing sequence using seven lighting trucks, each covering roughly two city blocks, several of the "Batman" movies, "Minority Report" (2002), "The Terminal" (Spielberg, starring Tom Hanks, 2003), "Open Range" (2003), "The Haunted Mansion" (2003), "Friday Night Lights" (2004), "Paparazzi" (2004), "Spiderman 3" (2006), "Alvin & the Chipmunks" (2007), "Twilight (2008), "Tenacious D: The Pick of Destiny" (2006), "Night at the Museum" (2006), "Die Hard 4" (2007), "Evan Almighty" (2007), "Transformers" (2007-2013), "Twilight" (2008), "Gone in Sixty Seconds" (2000), "Iron Man 2" (2009-2010), "Blindside" (2009), "The Hangover" (2009-2012), "Bridesmaids" (2010), "Footloose" (2010), "Men In Black" (2011), "The Internship" (2013), "Terminator Genisys" (2015), "A Quiet Place (2017), "Black Panther" (2017), "Creed 2" (2018), "Ford v Ferrari" (2018), "A Quiet Place 2" (2019), "The Conjuring 3" (2019), "Beverly Hills Cop 4" (2022), "Twisters" (2023-2024), "Lioness" (2024), and many more. Every once in a while, the impressive and handsome Night Lights trucks even make it onto the shows they are lighting, with one of the most prominent appearances in "Paparazzi" (2004).

Night Lights trucks at "Jurassic Park", 1992, Universal Studios, California.

Night Lights truck at "Pirates of the Caribbean, The Curse of the Black Pearl," Bahamas, 2003

Television shows include "Stranger Things," "America's Got Talent," "Animal Kingdom," "Bones," "Bosch," "Criminal Minds," "CSI," "The Walking Dead," "Gillmore Girls," "Ghost Whisperer," "Glee," "Good Morning America," "Grey's Anatomy," "International Surf Festival," "Leverage," "MacGyver," "Melrose Place," "Modern Family," "Monk," "NCIS," "Numbers," "Outer Range," "Parenthood," "SWAT," "The Voice," "This is Us," "Ugly Betty," "Yellowstone," and "90210," to name just a few.

Night Lights has significant expertise in lighting diverse sporting events, ranging from Olympic Track and Swim promotions to Super Bowl Commercials, local high school games, lifeguard competitions, swimming, off-road racing, motocross, lacrosse, cricket, and hockey.

Superbowl XLVII, New Orleans, Louisiana – Jackson Square 2013
Photo provided by Bill Brennan

A particularly unique project included an international outdoor ice hockey competition on a custom-built rink on the 18th fairway of the Edgewood Tahoe Resort during the 2021 COVID shutdowns. Their primary role was to ensure consistent lighting levels, compensating for shadows, overcast conditions, or nighttime play. When daytime games were suspended due to slushy ice, Night Lights illuminated the televised games at night as ice conditions improved.

Night Lights by Bebee trucks at Lake Tahoe for NHL, 2021
Photo provided by Night Lights by Bebee

Beyond entertainment, the company has been involved in numerous high-profile events. Night Lights provided large-area, high-intensity lighting for the press and media documenting NASA Space Shuttle landings on the salt flats in the Mojave Desert at Edwards Air Force Base. Bruce's prior top-secret military clearance granted him access to the secure area. Operationally, the lighting job was straightforward. Bruce was used to working on high-profile jobs and making them seem routine, when in fact there was nothing routine about taking his place for another piece of history. He sees most things he's done as "normal", though there is clearly nothing normal about what he's accomplished.

Operators for Night Lights are highly skilled. Bruce and Mitzi's youngest son, Junior, started with Bebee Generators in 1989 at age 18. He worked with Mitzi in the office and Bruce in the shop, working his way up to delivering and operating generators until Bebee Generators was sold in 1992. Shortly thereafter, Junior became proficient as a driver and operator with Night Lights by Bebee. Bruce recalls his namesake, "Junior showed great skill as a crane operator, and the clients on location all loved him." Bruce is proud of Junior's expertise, demonstrated while working for both Bebee companies. After Night Lights, he became a generator operator on location for multiple TV series and films. He is still successfully doing so today. In true generational form, Junior introduced his wife, Julie, and son, Shea, into the film industry as well.

In 2005, the catastrophic La Conchita landslide destroyed dozens of homes. It killed ten people in a small coastal neighborhood near Highway 1, South of Santa Barbara, California. ABC's "Good Morning America" contracted Night Lights by Bebee to provide lighting for their news coverage over three days. Bruce's son, Junior, was the operator and arrived around 10:30–

11:00 p.m. Pacific, earlier than the planned midnight call time. Because the site was dangerously dark and rescue work had been halted for safety reasons, Junior partially raised the light rack and turned on a few lights from off the highway. Rescuers saw the illumination, requested full lighting, and resumed operations. About twenty minutes later, they reportedly retrieved a woman from the rubble.

VENTURA COUNTY
FIRE PROTECTION DISTRICT

BOB ROPER
County Fire Chief

165 Durley Avenue
Camarillo, CA 93010-8586
(805) 389-9710
FAX (805) 388-4364

January 31, 2005

Mr. Bruce Bebee
NIGHT LIGHTS
2301 E Gladwick Street
Rancho Dominguez, CA 90220

Dear Mr. Bebee:

I would like to thank you for providing assistance and support to Ventura County during the La Conchita incident. This was an unprecedented incident in our county's history. The USGS now lists this incident as the largest life loss due to a landslide in U.S. history.

Your help by providing lighting for three days assisted in our search and rescue efforts and made our job easier. The vehicle, donated by "ABC Good Morning America," and your Driver Technician on scene, Bruce Bebee, Jr., were invaluable.

Please extend my sincere thanks to your staff. Your commitment made a difference, and I want you to know how much your assistance was appreciated by our department and the citizens of Ventura County.

Sincerely,

BOB ROPER
Fire Chief

One of Bruce's long-standing clients at Night Lights by Bebee is American Broadcasting Company (ABC). In addition to several sporting events, Night Lights was hired to provide lighting of iconic U.S. landmarks for ABC's "Seven Wonders of America" in May 2008. For this special series on "Good Morning America", Bruce's company lit several landmarks for early-morning live broadcasts. At the Golden Gate Bridge, they positioned a lighting truck at each end of the bridge and illuminated the full span for a 4 a.m. California live segment (7 a.m. New York). At the Grand Canyon Skywalk, they used three trucks to light roughly a mile along the rim and a mile and a half across the canyon, enabling visibility at 4 a.m. In New York, they lit the Statue of Liberty, again timed for a 7 a.m. live broadcast. Other wonders identified in the program included the National Mall in Washington, D.C., the Arctic National Wildlife Refuge in Alaska, the South Dakota Badlands, and the Saturn V Rocket in Huntsville, Alabama. According to records, viewers were asked to vote for an eighth wonder, with the Grand Canyon winning and appearing on the list twice.

Lighting The Golden Gate Bridge
Photo Credit Night Lights by Bebee, 2008

Lighting of the Grand Canyon
Photo Credit Night Lights by Bebee, 2008

Airport and aviation-related lighting for commercials and films calls for special considerations. On more than one occasion, Night Lights provided specialized lighting at airports, including LAX. For safety, this involved installing rotating light beacons atop the 120-foot-high booms so pilots could see the trucks on the tarmac. The work required balancing aviation safety with cinematographic needs, working directly on airport property, and adapting equipment for height and visibility constraints.

The lighting company continued to thrive until 2008. At that time, the housing financial crisis caused an industry-wide slowdown, as the movie industry's health is tied to the health of financial markets. Says Bruce, "If the market's doing well, then the industry's booming. If the market is crashing or money is expensive, then the industry is slow." It was during this time that Bruce and I met. It's a love story for another chapter. However, as the film industry partially stabilized in the market around

2010, additional business challenges began to emerge.

The Hollywood movie industry hit another downward trend. By 2018, technological advances made cameras more light-sensitive, reducing the demand for the high-power lights that were Night Lights' specialty, leading to downsizing from sixteen to nine trucks. Additionally, political and economic challenges of operating in Hollywood itself caused much of the film industry to leave California. Changes in emission and heavy equipment laws were making it increasingly expensive to operate in California, especially during an industry downturn amid rising real estate expenses. In response to the industry shifting towards the Eastern United States, Bruce had already moved some of his equipment to Georgia, and we had already purchased a nice home on a greenbelt in Austin, Texas. The goal was to relocate some of his trucks to a business-friendly state closer to his Night Lights clients.

Bruce had said many times that it would be his dream to have his shop only 500 feet from the house. That would allow him to tinker anytime, any day, especially as he approached retirement. We quickly found ourselves owning a home on nineteen acres in the Texas Hill Country, where Bruce had an 11,000-square-foot shop built within about four months. The Bebee Ranch, as we call it, is another bucket list item checked off.

In 2017, a realtor walked into the Gladwick shop with a buyer willing to pay what Bruce felt was a fair price for the property, so he accepted the offer, decided to downsize, and moved more equipment out of state, closer to his client's needs. The sale of Gladwick proved pivotal. It funded the purchase of additional out-of-state rental properties and a light industrial property for his Georgia shop (June 2020). For a while, he moved the California shop to a rental property in Whittier before finally making a more permanent switch to utilizing the Bebee Ranch in Texas as his main hub.

The rental properties funded by the sale of Gladwick provided crucial cash flow during the COVID shutdowns and subsequent industry strikes. Bruce recalls, "Out of three years, our industry basically was down a solid year and a half of literally no work. If it wasn't for the revenue that I received from my rental properties, I would probably have wound up out of business." Because Bruce was always mindful of cash flow and had diversified his income, he was able to keep his employees paid during the mandated closures, reinforcing a strong sense of loyalty and responsibility. About the COVID experience, Bruce emphasized, "I was not about to allow my people, who are like family, starve or lose their homes. It just wasn't going to happen. So anyway, we got through COVID, and I have some very loyal people who work for me." Bruce once again demonstrated resilience and practical risk management in the face of adversity.

Night Lights is still operating out of three locations today, with its main shop in the Texas Hill Country on the Bebee Ranch, a shop in Georgia, and a yard and administrative office in the Los Angeles area. The trucks still serve locations throughout the United States and beyond, making the ranch a convenient central hub in the countryside for moving them wherever they are needed.

After roughly two decades of loyal service, the closing of the main Night Lights shop in California marked the end of an era with one of Bruce's most trusted employees, Edmond Watson (Ed). Bruce explains, "I knew I could set up a project for Ed and he'd do it, no fuss, no drama. He was really a good welder with mechanical skills, very easy to get along with, and trusted to oversee the shop when neither Ken nor I could be there. He was capable of taking care of whatever was needed in our absence. Ed stayed with me until June of 2024, when we finally shut down the shop in California." Though it's said that Ed has seen the rougher side of life, he is a beautiful soul to be around. He visited the Bebee Ranch around the holidays, just after he retired. We shifted his welding skills from metal to icing to make Santa sleighs out of candy canes and MilkyWay bars for his grandchildren. Always a joy, he even helped hang Christmas lights on the porch. Ed is retired now, but is remembered as much for his loyalty as for his technical skills and friendly attitude.

CHAPTER SEVEN

Hard Work Pays Off

Enjoy Life

Bruce and Mitzi's life together was defined by a relentless work ethic, especially after they founded Bebee Generators in 1977. The first four years of building their future with Bebee Generators were predominantly a time of noses to the grindstone, as well as the excitement that comes with the possibilities and success of providing for the family. It established the foundational work ethic and sacrifice that defined their early married life and business, setting them up for later travel as a hard-earned reward, including multiple cruises to Hawaii and Alaska for fun, as well as two trips together in Costa Rica.

Bebee Generators had become very profitable. In 1986, U.S. tax laws changed, and regional incentive programs favored investments in Costa Rica. The entrepreneur Bebee couple invested in a property slated for development in Costa Rica. In 1987, the incentive program was canceled, and the mismanaged company, which had multiple partners besides the Bebees, defaulted on the payments. With the help of his Costa Rican attorney, Bruce made a deal with the banker for 20 cents on the dollar and became the sole owner of 640 acres near Lake Arenal.

Roughly 225 acres of the property consisted of a macadamia farm, which Bruce hired locals to operate. Realizing the costs were overriding the profits, they switched the property to cattle ranching, with approximately 1,800 head. They cycled the cattle by selling 150 adults and purchasing 150 calves each month, making about $30 to $50 per head: enough to offset the farm's operating costs. Bruce recalls, “It was not a very good investment, but when people asked what we were doing in Costa Rica, we used to just say we were supporting a village—because yeah, that was about it.” They kept that property, and Bruce enjoyed frequent trips to Costa Rica for about 20 years before selling it in 2006. To this day, Bruce loves Costa Rica and the experiences shared there.

A significant turning point came through their business relationship with the Hilton Hotel, which introduced them to a world of travel and entertainment centered around Las Vegas, a city Mitzi fell in love with. Playing the slot machines was her chosen form of release and entertainment. The Hilton connection encouraged Bruce’s adventurous side, shining light on the many layers of his identity—more than a mechanic, not just a businessman, but a pilot and outdoorsman moving in elite circles.

Bruce recalls many adventurous trips with the Hilton group. There were several Alaska fishing trips from which Bruce was able to stock family and friends’ freezers with salmon for months on end. He and (and sometimes Mitzi) enjoyed being guests at the Hilton Ranch, which often involved sporting activities such as shooting and hunting.

Bruce H. Bebee and a 63.3-pound King salmon, Waterfall Resort, July 15, 2002

Mitzi loved Las Vegas, so the two decided to relocate there in 1994. Besides, Night Lights was already operating out of Los Angeles, and this gave Bruce yet another reason to fly his plane back and forth. Bruce tells a story about a nice senior community in North Las Vegas that had just started a program allowing custom modifications to its new homes. Eager to create his dream home on the golf course, Bruce borrowed a set of blueprints overnight and came back the next day with multiple changes drawn up. Their new home there, completed in 1994, was expanded from

2400 to 3200 square feet, including the first three-car garage in the development, an office, a redesigned kitchen, and other unique customizations. Bruce had fun designing the house, but he's pretty sure the builder stopped offering custom changes after the Bebee house was completed. The couple lived there from 1994 to 1998, while still running their business, Night Lights by Bebee, out of Los Angeles County. It was easy going back and forth since they had living quarters in their Gardena shop.

Bruce H. Bebee moving his 421 Twin engine 1980 Cessna out of the hangar in Las Vegas, NV, 1995. This was his third out of four planes he owned.

The couple often held family reunions at the Las Vegas Hilton, inviting their kids (including their kids' friends), siblings, and close friends to join in on New Year's Eve and other high-end celebrations hosted by the hotel. It was at one of these Hilton Las Vegas events when Bruce and Mitzi were invited to attend Mohammed Ali's birthday party.

Bruce H. Bebee and Mitzi Bebee, Las Vegas, NV

There was always something to do in Las Vegas, even for Bruce's adventurous side. Whether it was riding motorcycles with his friend Lloyd or attending car racing events together, there was always something fun. Bruce, his sons, in-laws, and friends drove Formula 1 race cars at the Mario Andretti Racing School, testing their skills to see just how fast they could go, achieving speeds of 150 to 160 mph on a banked track. Says Bruce, "It seems like every other week we had guests at our house because of the adventure available in Las Vegas." Eventually, Vegas life grew old, and the couple moved back to Huntington Beach, where they purchased their final home together.

Granddaughters Jenna and Rebecca recall fun game evenings with Mitzi (Meme) and Bruce (Papa) playing Rummikub, watching the "X Files," and eating orange candy slices as the overnight entertainment when their family came from out of state to visit. This underscores the significance of simple family time separate from the glamor and allure of the prior home in Las Vegas. Bruce appreciates that he and Mitzi spent their final years together in Huntington Beach, where they were blessed to have a home on the harbor with a beach to welcome their guests. This is where they entertained not only intimate family game nights, but also hosted large potluck holiday parties with friends and family, enjoying the annual Boat Parade of Lights that cruised past the backyard every December.

Mitzi loved people and hugged everyone she met. She loved her coffee and cigarettes. She also loved playing games of all kinds: board games, card games, slots, and video Poker. Donna reminisces, "One of my favorite games we played was Cribbage, and she was so good at it." Bruce agrees, "Mitzi won most of the time. She had a system. She told me she used the same system in playing video poker, and I honestly never fully understood it, but it seemed to work well for her. I used to joke with her that beating me all the time in Cribbage should be considered spousal abuse. We played Cribbage quite a bit."

Bruce carries a life philosophy of surrounding oneself with upbeat, intelligent, capable people, avoiding "downers," and avoiding the trap of wanting to be the smartest person in the room. Instead, he recommends adopting a growth mindset and wearing a smile to attract upbeat people into your life. He states, "We learn from our mistakes and from people who are brighter than we are. They are there to help." He intertwines friendship, work, travel, and a values-driven approach to life and business. He is a man who finds enjoyment in even the simplest routines, shared curiosity, adventure, and popcorn.

Bruce maintains numerous friendships with people he met on the job. One of those was his best friend, Larry Boyle. This friendship was forged during work on ABC motocross events, where Bruce provided generators and Larry provided security through a firm he started with a fellow retired Long Beach police officer. Larry was studying for his attorney's license and also worked in real estate to pay the bills. It was Larry who sold Bruce a six-unit apartment building in Long Beach. Bruce recalls, "That investment didn't lose money, but it was a pain, so we sold it after two years." In the meantime, he and Larry became solid friends and discovered they had a lot in common. For one, they both enjoyed popcorn. "I think it was every Wednesday, we would go out to the movies. He and I both enjoyed popcorn at the movies, but neither of our wives did. So it tended to work out very well." After the movie, they'd go out for a meal or coffee, and talk about business and life. Larry passed his bar exam and became a prosecuting attorney for Los Angeles County. He was an intelligent man and always pleasant to be around.

Bruce recalls his first set of golf clubs suddenly getting some play when Mitzi signed him up to play in a tournament with Larry on a team of four. Never having taken up the game, Bruce took two lessons to prepare himself for the tournament at the Navy Golf Course in Los Alamitos, California. The course was later recognized as the 18-hole golf facility where famous golfer Tiger Woods played in his youth, coincidentally around the same time Bruce played in this tournament. On the third hole, a par 3, Larry jokingly asked Bruce about his plan for sinking the ball. Bruce described, "I'm just going to hit it to the slope on the left, and it will just roll in." And that's precisely what transpired. Bruce chuckles, "After that, they thought I was a ringer! With two lessons and one game. Yep." In that moment, he was one with the golf club, never to be repeated. It's his one and only Hole in One!

Larry and Bruce were best friends, and even traveled together for two Costa Rica adventures, ostensibly to check out the ranch investment. Memories of these travels include vivid stories of a reservation mishap due to a name mix-up ("Mr. Bruce"), strenuous hotel climbs, visits to Bruce's macadamia ranch, and memorable meals, like a whole fish served poolside.

They explored Costa Rica and were taking life easy at a U-shaped hotel with a swim-up bar/restaurant in the center. Bruce describes, "It was one of those places you literally had to go in the water to get to. Larry ordered off the lunch menu. In contrast, Bruce inquired about possibilities with the bartender, "Last night when I was in the restaurant, we saw them serve a whole fish on a platter. It looked really good. Is there any way I can have that for lunch?"

The bartender said yes and put in the order. "Larry received his lunch first, a poolside burger or hotdog with fries. Two or three minutes later, here comes the chef with a fish on a platter," Bruce grins, "And he's walking out, holding it in front of him with two hands, and he's walking around to an entrance that leads into the bar area. They bring it right over and set it down in front of me. And I swear, everybody in the place was looking at me like, 'Who is this guy?' My only comment, I turned to Larry, and I go, 'life is really good'. So, it was. And the fish was really good, too." The two got a chuckle out of that, and Bruce has never found a fish to match that again. This incident was so memorable, and the fish was so good, that even after many years had passed and we were in Costa Rica on our honeymoon, Bruce and I attempted to find that U-shaped hotel with the swim-up bar, but to no avail.

CHAPTER EIGHT

Find Your People

It's a logical strategy to surround yourself in everyday business with people you enjoy being around. Bruce's pride is not just in his own accomplishments, but also in his ability to build and lead a capable, hardworking team, many of whom go on to succeed in their own ventures. He is a leader who respects and appreciates his employees. His business success is intertwined with the quality of the people he hires, and he speaks of them with great gratitude for being part of his life. There are too many amazing employees to mention in detail, but it is fun to call out a few for the memories they inspire. With the time and passion required to achieve his mechanical innovations in business, it's no wonder that Bruce's most trusted and capable employees become close friends, often like family.

Friend and long-term employee, Brad Campbell, was originally Bruce and teenage son Bruce Jr.'s martial arts instructor who owned a local dojo. It's notable that witnessing another student's catastrophic knee injury during a jump in a black belt test crystallized Bruce's priorities as a business owner. The potential for injuries was not something he was willing to risk his business for, so he quit attending the dojo. A couple of years later, after Bruce and Mitzi moved to Las Vegas, Brad was debating a career shift and approached Bruce for a job. Bruce's response was positive, "You're a fifth-degree black belt. Anybody who has that determination and drive to achieve that is someone I can work with. I can teach you any and everything I need for you to become one of my operators." Thus began a nearly three-decade working relationship, demonstrating Bruce's philosophy of hiring for character and teachability. Brad started in the shop, earned his Class A heavy truck driver's license within six months, and became an operator for Night Lights around 1997–1998. Bruce describes him as calm, reliable, and consistently effective, with no problems or drama. Brad is retired now, but his presence became part of Bruce's team culture.

Bruce has a knack for finding or reconnecting with acquaintances at just the right time. He listened, found out where they were in their lives, and invited them into his world of lighting. This not only benefited his own business but also fostered meaningful engagement among the people he hired. He found that some of his most trusted employees didn't necessarily operate for him solely for financial reasons. They were often seeking their next chapter of connection or fun. It then became Bruce's goal to equip them with the right training and tools to succeed.

Bebee shares a long, serendipitous relationship with Bruce Bradford, a key employee and an old acquaintance from when Bebee was just fifteen years old. Their connection began in high school, when both worked at the local grocery store, Arico's Market. They had occasional contact throughout different life stages (high school reunions, conversations about generators for the fire department, etc.) before a chance encounter at a gym in Hawthorne, California, reconnected them decades later. By then, Bradford was a retired Fire Department Deputy Commander. Bebee recalls Bradford volunteering to learn how to build, maintain, and operate the Night Lights trucks without compensation as he apprenticed before being sent out on location.

Demonstrating outstanding character and willingness to learn from the bottom up, Bradford solidified his value long before he ever drew a paycheck. A strong work ethic, exemplified by Bradford's meticulous, firefighter-honed discipline, made him a standout employee, often polishing the trucks when he was on location. Bebee used to joke with Bradford, "We'll just start you off at truck number one. You can keep going through all the trucks and then start over again." Bradford worked nearly three decades for Night Lights. Bebee recounts with the highest compliment a boss can give, "I would have loved to have had a couple of him. Bruce Bradford's always been very, very easy to get along with, very pleasant and a great employee."

Ken Inglet is a loyal friend and employee who worked as the shop foreman at Night Lights for over two decades. Ken came to the company around 2000, when Junior was working for Night Lights. He and Junior knew each other through their shared love of playing pool. Bruce and Ken became close friends, built on trust and defined by shared interests and mutual respect. "Ken had electrical knowledge, had been in the Navy as an electrician, and had a Class A driver's license. He had all the skills I needed for someone with the trucks, and eventually I made him foreman of my shop. He had the knowledge and the skills to do just about anything." Ken's high level of technical competence allowed Bruce to focus more on growth and oversight of Night Lights. Ken was a skilled operator who understood the whole system on the trucks and helped build the later Night Lights trucks.

It's good to have a few bucket list items to dream about. It's even better when you actually accomplish those items with friends and family. Five men, consisting of Bruce, Ken, Lloyd Campbell, Bruce's brother-in-law, Gary Kellogg, and Bruce's brother, Gary Bebee, adventured together on a Harley motorcycle trip at the Sturgis Motorcycle Rally in 2007. In classic road trip style, four of the men loaded up a toy trailer with their shiny Harleys to leave their daily lives in California behind for the open road adventure to South Dakota. Their final comrade, Lloyd, rode in from Idaho to join them. The friends were ready to take on Sturgis.

Bruce smiles, "Everybody has to ride the strip. They've got two rows of motorcycles down the middle of the road, then also motorcycles on either side for about five blocks. We went three blocks in about 20 to 25 minutes. It's just a foot or two here, a foot or two there. You just keep moving very slowly because it's so crowded. It's nothing but motorcycles. All I can remember is my legs starting to get tired, shaking, and burning from the heat of the motor, because your legs are always out, balancing when you're only moving a foot or two at a time, letting the clutch out, moving a little bit. Then, letting the clutch out, moving a little bit. That's what I remember about it. I finally turned off and said, I've had enough of this abuse." Bruce chuckles at himself with a sigh of relief that he survived the quintessential but grueling motorcycle crawl down the strip, surrounded by a sea of chrome and leather. "But anyway, we had a good time. It was a lot of fun!" The five friends rode to Mount Rushmore, the Crazy Horse Memorial, Rapid City, Needles Highway/ Iron Mountain Rd, and all around the beautiful countryside. Bruce particularly recalls the thrill and challenge of Needles Highway, "...it was a single lane twisty road up to where you actually went through a tunnel... and it took us all the way up to the peak." It embodied the spirit of exploration and adventure that defined the trip—it wasn't just about the crowded rally, but about discovering hidden gems together.

Needles Hwy during the Sturgis Motorcycle Rally trip, South Dakota, 2007
Left to right: Bruce H. Bebee, Gary Bebee, Gary Kellogg, Ken Inglet
Photo taken by Lloyd Campbell

Bruce kept his Harley for several years. I recall him carefully covering it in a safe place in the garage, and I knew it held special memories with friends. When it came time to sell the motorcycle, another friendship was waiting to happen. The buyer, Jim Kiatos, had searched high and low for such a beautiful machine and was eager to acquire it. Beyond that, he was very intrigued by the Night Lights truck fleet he witnessed during the transaction and asked Bruce for a job. Jim already held a Class A license, the ability to operate a crane, and a healthy respect for electricity. He's been a Night Lights operator ever since. Bruce appreciates Jim as an employee and friend, "He's intelligent, respectful, easy to get along with, and a very good operator. He takes good care of the equipment, being mindful to check on the trucks, even if they aren't going out on a job." Life is interesting, and you just never know where you will find your next friend, outstanding employee, or both.

Bruce met Lloyd Campbell in 1974, toward the beginning of his career in the film industry. Lloyd was an "earth dam engineer". Bruce teases, "We always dropped the 'earth' part of that description." They built a profound personal and professional relationship with Lloyd becoming one of Bruce's closest friends. Their connection was rooted in a shared engineering mindset and a powerful work ethic. Lloyd began working for Bebee Generators in 1984 as a generator operator. The two men also partnered on a major business venture—building a Chevron fuel station in Boise, Idaho.

Lloyd had a piece of property at the main junction of Beacon Light Rd and Hwy 55 in Boise, Idaho, where he built the Chevron station with a convenience store. Bruce basically financed the construction, and Lloyd built it. He literally designed it and then fabricated a 4,000-square-foot building in Bruce's Gardena shop. He did all the welding, built the structure, rented a flatbed trailer, and carted the massive deconstructed building all the way up to Boise to create the Chevron store, which is still there today. Bruce proudly commends Lloyd's work, "He actually received an award for building such an energy-efficient building, and in a little over a year, his store became the highest Chevron producer in the area." However, the lifestyle of a station owner was exhausting. Lloyd was working seven days a week, had gone through 45 employees in one year, and was ready to sell. Bruce recalls Lloyd's frustration as a business owner, "I hire people, and they don't even show up." Lloyd's experience highlights the limits of hard work and the harsh realities of running a service business. They sold the station, bringing Lloyd back to Los Angeles to operate trucks for Night Lights.

Their friendship extended far beyond work, involving numerous shared vacations: the Sturgis Rally, Alaska fishing trips, Las Vegas parties, Hawaii, and family gatherings with their wives, Mitzi and Mary Lynn. Bruce particularly recalls their Hawaii trips. "He and I rented motorcycles in Maui, and the girls had a car. We would ride in and meet them wherever they wanted to go for lunch or dinner." It was a perfect balance of male camaraderie, independence, and comfortable partnership with their wives. However, it's also true that the two men often ran ideas past each other on how to resolve mechanical issues, reportedly driving their wives insane when mechanical discussion drowned out all other conversation. Despite very different educational paths, Bruce and Lloyd had an intellectual and temperamental bond, with their friendship based as much on shared thinking as on shared work. It was a great friendship, but it was cut way too short. After 24 years as a loyal employee and 34 years building meaningful memories together, Lloyd passed away within 14 months of Mitzi's passing. It was an immense personal loss for Bruce.

CHAPTER NINE

Layers of Security

Real Estate Wisdom, Diversification, Survival

Bruce doesn't believe in relying on a single stream of income. Security, to him, is something you build in layers. Bruce fundamentally believes in real estate investing. He enjoys the hunt as much as the financial security he feels with owning. “I've known that real estate is the only way you literally can retire when you get older. Because if you buy real estate and hold it, it just keeps increasing in value. It's like forced savings.” It was the sale of their first family home and rental property that provided the capital to build their first generators. In addition to their residences, Mitzi and Bruce purchased multiple properties for business, leisure, and investment purposes. Later in life, a key family practice established by Mitzi and Bruce was to help their kids by providing downpayments for their first home purchases.

Bruce didn't always keep the real estate investments, but each proved to be an experience to build on. Sometimes they were just fun, sometimes they were outright inconvenient, and a few led to pivotal moments when real estate provided the financing to develop or sustain business goals. Let's run through a few investments to illustrate a pattern of taking calculated risks, assessing viability, and adjusting accordingly.

It was the sale of their first family home and rental property that provided the capital to build their first generators. This changed the entire trajectory of their life.

Bruce's best friend, Larry Boyle, was the selling agent on a six-unit apartment building in Long Beach. Ever the entrepreneur, Bruce purchased the property in 1981 but quickly decided it was a poor investment. The area wasn't great; tenants didn't pay on time, maintenance costs were high, and the management team didn't stay on top of things. He didn't lose money, but it was absolutely no fun, and he sold it in 1983, all the wiser for it.

Likewise, the investment in Costa Rica was not only an experience of property investment under poor management, but also a change in international incentives. Fortunately, Bruce was able to turn that one into a fun adventure with good travel stories and an unexpected knowledge of raising cattle. I'm sure the locals he supported appreciated him as well.

Bruce and Mitzi purchased various personal properties like mountain homes in Mammoth and Wrightwood, and a condo in Palm Springs, all of which he recalls were mostly intended for fun with their kids. But she was tired of owning multiple properties and the attention they required, so all but the river house in Parker (the family favorite) were sold after a couple of years.

The Chevron station was more about supporting his

friend, Lloyd, than anything else. In the end, it's a point of pride to know that Lloyd won awards and that Bruce was part of it. It's also a fun fact that the station is still there. If you live in Boise, please check it out and know that the "Forrest Gump of Mechanics" played a role.

Unjaded by prior purchases and still holding a fascination with real estate, Bruce purchased six properties in the San Bernardino area at auction in 2010. He converted all the properties into rentals, which worked out great for a while, until would-be squatters and nonpaying renters tried even his steady patience. He sold the California rental properties and was glad of it. With the California rental properties no longer a burden, Bruce moved his real estate ventures out of state. This was a pivotal moment in his real estate investments, as these were finally both profitable and efficient.

The purchase of the Gladwick property was the last property purchased with Mitzi. It was a gorgeous and extremely functional shop. The sale of this property proved pivotal in two ways. The funds allowed Nightlights by Bebee to operate more effectively across multiple locations by funding a smaller shop in the Los Angeles area, purchasing a shop in Georgia, and maintaining the Bebee Ranch shop. It funded the purchase of additional out-of-state rental properties, providing crucial cash flow during industry-wide shutdowns. This literally kept the business alive. Bruce's belief that real estate ownership provides layers of security proved true.

Bruce is a proponent of multiple income streams and has advice for real estate investors. In addition to exploring the option of 1031 exchanges when selling rental properties, he recommends, "Hire a good, reliable company to manage your properties, which takes the burden off of owning property and trying to control it yourself. They handle all the maintenance, tenants, everything." He now prefers light industrial property over residential rentals, and advises, "Consider industrial properties because the people who own businesses usually take better care of the property. It's their place of business, and they typically take more personal responsibility. Conversely, rental housing can quickly be destroyed or fall behind on rent, and all the tenants lose is their deposit. Sometimes they'll just strip the house before they leave." Either way, Bruce recommends purchasing property when you are young, or on a 15-year mortgage that you can pay off before you retire. "That way, you've just set yourself up for a more comfortable retirement."

CHAPTER TEN

Permission And The Prayer

Just three days before Mitzi passed in March 2009, she gave Bruce a selfless gift—one that he didn't yet understand. Mitzi told Bruce they needed to talk, "You know you will outlive me. If something happens to me, you should get married again. You love being married." Bruce was caught off guard by her request and asked if she had anyone in particular in mind. He had no idea at the time how serious her health was declining, as she refused to talk about it or go to a doctor. But apparently, she knew and was giving him permission to live life. This is grace in the most difficult of seasons, and it was a beautiful gift from Mitzi. It shows her deep love and respect for Bruce: she didn't want him to be alone. After forty years of marriage and building a life together, she wanted him to be happy.

It was April of 2009 when I saw a shooting star while on a short Spring Break vacation in Palm Desert with my daughter, Patricia, and close friends, Mary and

Charlie. I quietly started a conversation with God that went something like this:

"Dear God,

Please help me understand my path. I am blessed and grateful for a beautiful daughter, loving family, and very loyal friends. You know about the struggles of co-parenting with Patricia's dad. Patricia tells me things with him are getting more and more complicated, so you know I will support her in addressing that. I am always busy balancing work with parenting. I don't want us to miss out on the fun to be had during her childhood. It just doesn't seem like single guys my age have their act together, so is it even worth my time to date? If I do date, is there a man who isn't intimidated by the fact that I am totally capable of taking care of myself, but who still wants to take care of me? How about a man who is financially responsible and not waiting for my income or my house to relieve his own financial stress? I love kids, but is there a man who is more excited about what a great lifelong partnership we will have than he is about what a great mom I will be to his kids? Or even a man who is financially stable and doesn't spend every dime he has on toys or lifestyle beyond his means? Don't even get me started on a man who has addictions or any kind of substance abuse… been there, done that… wouldn't wish that on anyone. I want a man I can respect. And what about a man with kids who will be safe around my young daughter, and no crazy ex-spouse that I need to worry about? I'm seriously looking for someone with little baggage… Oh gosh, I have baggage." I sighed for a moment. "I feel like the only way I'm going to find this kind of man is if he is a widower, and I wouldn't wish that on anyone."

And just then, I kid you not, don't think I'm crazy…. I heard a voice say, "There is." It caught me completely off guard, and I somewhat nervously freaked myself out, wondering how I could have possibly heard that voice that was… distinctly female! So, I quickly responded, “Never mind, Lord. I’m good. Amen. Good night.”

The following week, I was at the local gym after work. Donning my baggy gray sweats, I was getting myself in shape to chaperone Patricia’s eighth-grade class on a field trip to Yosemite. A tall gentleman sat down next to me on the bicycle. He said hello and started a conversation. He was a successful business owner who had just lost his wife. He was exercising in the gym every day after work as a coping mechanism for the tremendous grief he was experiencing.

Bruce chimes in, “I was going to the gym two hours a day, every day, just as a way of working out the stress and loss, and I knew quite a few of the people there. Obviously, friends and family were offering sympathy and so forth—I was not looking to meet anybody at the moment. I’d had people trying to fix me up, and it was just too soon after Mitzi passed, just five or six weeks prior. As I sat on the bike, I started a general conversation about being smarter than the machine that I was on. I've always been a bit self-conscious about my lack of formal education, so I asked her what she did for a living and found out she was an engineering geologist. My thoughts were, well, I'm basically an engineer myself, so we are on even grounds. Upon further questioning, I discovered that she graduated from the Colorado School of Mines in geophysical engineering. And that's when I said to myself, Bruce, it's time to get up and walk away. This girl's way too smart for you.”

We are both grateful he stayed on that bike, because eventually he posed a couple of questions that changed our lives forever. “I’d like to ask you a couple of questions, but before I do, I want you to know that I’m hoping your answer is yes. Please don’t be offended, but are you over 50 and single?" I was in my late 40s, so my reply was, "Almost and yes." Bruce confidently asked, "Then would you go to dinner with me?" To which I warned him, "Yes, I'd go to dinner with you, but I'm not sure you want to go there--my life is complicated." Smiling back, he offered, "Of course, your life is complicated, you are a single working mother. I'd still like to take you to dinner." So I said yes, but to lunch. He'd been at the gym going on three hours, and we said our goodbyes. He never asked for my phone number, so I let it go because I knew my life was going to get super busy over the next couple of months.

However, that night on the phone, I did tell my sister Karalyn about this really nice man I met. She immediately began vetting him online in real time as I told her details. She confirmed, "Everything he told you checks out. The website for his business features a tribute to his wife, who recently passed away. I think he is who he says he is." I backpedaled with excuses, "I'm just so busy, and this coming month is complicated, helping Patricia address issues with her dad. It's going to take everything I have to get that right. Besides, I am not sure about the age difference." The question she posed to me next is one I am forever grateful for: "You are probably correct that he must be older than you, but if you like him, I highly recommend the happiness thing." Well, that stopped me in my tracks, and I knew she was absolutely right. I started watching for Bruce at every workout, but it was two weeks before we met again.

Bruce recalls going all the way home that night and thinking, "Wow, I really like her—intelligent, good-looking, somebody who's capable of taking care of herself. Mitzi had only passed away five or six weeks previously, but I thought, well, we'll see what lunch brings. And then I realized, I forgot to get her phone number. So anyway, the next day, unfortunately, I had to go out of town for business, and I was gone for about a week."

Once back in town, Bruce got right back to the gym, this time with intention, "Every day, I'd look around to see if I recognized her. And one day I was walking towards the bathroom—I'd just finished a two-hour workout—and she stepped in front of me and said, "Do you remember me?" And I said, "Yes." And I said, "Before you say another word, can I have your phone number?" And so, she gave it to me, and we agreed to go to lunch."

Our first date was lunch at Maggiano's Little Italy near my work. I'd cautioned him that I was super busy at work and only had forty-five minutes. It was true, I was busy… but after an hour, we were still conversing, and I assured him that I could stretch it out, which turned into an hour and a half. I knew at that lunch… this was a man I could respect. He truly loved his late wife, Mitzi. He was a veteran, and we were on the same page with so many values. He had adult children and grandchildren. He looked me straight in the eye when we spoke, and I knew he was a self-confident individual who knew who he was. He told me that he loved being married and wasn't looking for casual dating. He wanted to find someone who wanted to be married too. I appreciated his straightforward honesty, a sign of the integrity I know is deeply embedded in his persona. I went back to work, and I knew. I just knew… and the rest is history.

Bruce confesses with emotion, "One thing I've never told her—and a lot of people, you might be able to understand—was we were at lunch, sitting talking, and all that came into my mind was, I'd just like to reach over and kiss her. So, it's been that way ever since. We've been married now nearly sixteen years, and it's really been great." With tears developing, he looks me straight in the eyes, “I’m getting emotional here. I love you.”

“I love you too,” I whispered, tears of gratitude softening my voice, and turned off my recording device.

CHAPTER ELEVEN

Our Life

About six weeks into our dating relationship, I froze in thought, in gratitude, and almost in jaw-dropping silence; I recalled that night of prayer in Palm Desert. This man was exactly who I'd prayed for. God honors commitments, and He is good. Bruce gifted me an engagement ring at Christmas. We waited a year before getting married out of respect for grieving family members, especially Bruce's kids and grandchildren. We wanted to give our kids time to adjust to the idea that we'd fallen in love and planned to spend the rest of our lives together. We married in June 2010 and celebrated with a backyard reception on Huntington Harbor.

Our wedding reception, Huntington Beach, California, June 2010. Left to right: Rochelle, Minerva, Tom, Brooke, Wally, Donna, Gail, Bruce, Patricia, Rebecca, Kai, Jenna, Shea, Julie, Bruce Jr.

Though happy to find love again, Bruce was still grieving the death of his first wife, Mitzi. He also found himself overwhelmed by administrative duties and sought a competent office manager for Night Lights. It was a key turning point in which he had to restructure his company's operations after sustaining the heavy personal and professional loss of his life partner. He turned to me for assistance in finding someone. Cheryl and I knew each other as Girl Scout volunteers for years, and I trusted her in every way. It turned out to be a great professional match. Bruce recalls, "We worked to create systems and training cheat sheets to address the steep learning curve required of her as she stepped into such a critical time." To this day, Cheryl is a highly efficient, loyal, and trustworthy employee who has successfully learned the business operations so that Bruce can get back to the technical issues in the shop, his happy place. Cheryl runs administrative operations for three Night Lights business centers and handles customer relations. Personally, I am immensely proud and grateful for Cheryl's ability to rise to the occasion and help Bruce when she did. Her long-term tenure highlights her loyalty and competence as a highly trusted, invaluable employee.

Bruce and Mitzi had been empty nesters for years. Our marriage gave Bruce his fourth child, Patricia, who was 15 when we married. Entering into a marriage with a new teenage daughter raised the eyebrows of multiple friends who warned, "Are you out of your mind marrying a woman with a teenage kid?" But Bruce was confident that the three of us were a good match. After meaningful interactions with Patricia, he felt secure in the future. She was an active young lady, bringing youthful energy to the household. Bruce says, "I really enjoyed it. It was life-changing." There were "mind-blowing" musical theater performances, school projects, academics, and so many wonderful friends who became frequent visitors. Bruce was impressed by how talented, responsible, and respectful they all were, especially the Scout troop, which helped set up and clean up after gatherings.

Combined, we have four children. Just as Bruce welcomed two prior children when he met Mitzi, he welcomed Patricia with the same care and support as his own. In turn, I was blessed by the addition of his three adult children and seven grandchildren before the age of fifty. It's a fun fact that often blows people's minds if they don't know our story, especially once the great-grandchildren started arriving. Life is good!

Roughly two years into our marriage, we had the blessing of having our granddaughter, Brooke, move in with us. It was a time of compassion, support, healing, and added love in the household, with Bruce requiring only one thing: a hug at the end of the day. He now had two teenagers in the house, and it was life-changing for all of us. Brooke and Patricia became like sisters.

Brooke endeared herself to us with her sweet demeanor and willingness to challenge herself.

Normally known for his pragmatic, problem-solving, and leadership capacity, Bruce's back-to-back losses of wife Mitzi (2009) and best friend Lloyd (2010), as well as Larry's physical decline at the time (passed in 2015), highlighted a human vulnerability and prolonged season of grief and change for Bruce in the early years of our marriage. Though he maintained an exceptional presence during this time, I experienced his deep compassion and heart in ways that I believe many in his family have never witnessed. Yet, through this season, we grew more and more in love and gratitude for each other and the life we were building together.

It was through Brooke and close family friends Tom and Nancy Caruso that Bruce was introduced to the world of personal growth seminars. Always willing to learn and grow, Bruce was impressed by Brooke's personal growth unfolding before us and decided to check out the seminars for himself. In his first seminar, he discovered something about himself: he was angry at his closest circle (Mitzi and Lloyd) for "leaving him." Anger is known to be a common stage of grief. This seminar enabled Bruce to recognize it for what it was and release it. He came home with a smile on his face and decided to gift the seminar to his family and employees. His second breakthrough came in a subsequent seminar, where he set his next life goal: to read. In true Bruce style, he promptly found the resources to assist himself, committed himself to daily study after work, and became the family's most avid reader. After nearly 70 years struggling with the written word, he could READ. Thank you, Brooke. The ripple effect you started helped your grandfather heal and grow. We are never beyond growing, learning, or seeking help.

Bruce loves life. We share a love for travel and adventure. It's no wonder that our first trip together was a fishing trip in Alaska, complete with a float plane experience, of course. There was also an early camping trip to Rocky Mountain National Park with Patricia and my brother, Curt: a humorous account in which Bruce discovered just how proficient Patricia and I are at setting up camp, outpacing even my most proficient brother and Bruce's mechanical aptitudes. One can't be too certain, but this may have solidified my position as future marriage material.

We spent our honeymoon in Costa Rica, checking out many of Bruce's old stomping grounds, looking for the magical fish on a platter, riding zip lines, searching out wildlife (my joy), and hoping for the elusive volcano eruption he had promised.

Bruce has traveled all over the world and was there for history in the process. Today, our life together is different. He generously supports my bucket list, and we've been blessed to experience the joys of God's creation in truly memorable ways. As a pilot, he was excited that one of my early adult dreams was to fly an airplane. He rekindled that dream, and I took flight safety instruction before we took a grand trip flying his plane to Yellowstone. All the way, he pointed out how a safety-conscious pilot thinks and watches from the sky; and all the way, I pointed out the amazing geologic features below us. Bruce proved his excellent flying skills by landing in harsh wind conditions in West Yellowstone on that trip, with the air traffic control team coming out to commend him. Commenting that they didn't believe everyone would be so skilled, they shut down the runway minutes later.

Gail T. Bebee, Bruce H. Bebee, Patricia Cosulich
Alaska Mountain Biking Expedition, 2019

There were trips to Greece with the high school fine arts department, Hawaii adventures, more fishing, more Alaska, more Costa Rica, high school reunions, whale encounters, yurts on the beach in Mexico, Canada, Japan, National Parks, Antarctica, and multiple trips to see family across the United States. There were bears fishing in a river, penguins belly-sliding down slopes, whales showing off their calves, the ever-elusive moose eating grass, eagles fishing, sloths slothing, monkeys chasing, dolphins swimming, fawns wobbling, woodpeckers chirping, and fish jumping. It's an amazing world, and Bruce is up for it.

And just like anyone else, there are challenges along the way. Through all of it, Bruce has my back. It was Bruce who made sure to invite Patricia's father to family dinners following her musical theater performances and various award ceremonies. The last such dinner was an unanticipated gift of healing conversation just shortly before Patricia's dad passed away. Bruce provided solid real estate guidance to Patricia after her father and grandparents passed. Bruce's support also assured that Patricia and I were able to access specialized health care when we were hit with debilitating chronic lyme and mycotoxin illness. He bridged the gap between scholarship and college expenses for Patricia to achieve her academic goals. He opened our home to friends needing a place to recover from surgery, friends waiting for their house to be fixed, and college friends with summer jobs. He set aside space in the Bebee Ranch shop for my brother Curt to use as a woodshop to create amazing woodworking projects, and he created a win-win scenario for Curt to join us living at the ranch. The list of his generosity is long. Life is good.

Bruce H. Bebee and Gail T. Bebee at the end of a waterfall rappelling expedition, Costa Rica, 2017

While living in Huntington Beach, there were many gatherings, holidays with family, visits from friends, Boat Parade potlucks, birthday parties, biking along the beach, and so much more. Through it all, Bruce exemplifies the meaning of "we are social beings". He loves meeting new people wherever we go. We make new friends in RV parks, restaurants, on beach walks, and on bicycle rides. I love being married to this man of genuine kindness and generosity, and I appreciate his patience in searching out all wildlife, cool rocks, and pretty plants wherever we adventure.

One of Bruce's endearing qualities is his deep love of family. With siblings, kids, and grandkids spread across the country, it's a challenge to see them all in person. That means taking the initiative to make it happen as often as we can, even while he is still working and running his Night Lights business. More than once, Bruce has come home to tell me we are joining his brother, Brent, and sister-in-law, Toni, for a trip to Hawaii. These are treasured sibling/family trips. With a four-year age difference and Bruce joining the Air Force after high school, Brent and Bruce never spent as much time together as they have in these golden years. We absolutely appreciate and love them and their family: so many veterans—thank you for your service!

Bruce and his older brother, Gary, are close in age and often spent time together while growing up. As adults, they both ran businesses in Southern California, allowing them to regularly meet for lunch to talk shop or life in general. A former LAPD motor cop, Gary, rode with Bruce and the guys on their famous Sturgis adventure. It was so fun hearing the two brothers reminisce about times past as we rang in the New Year with him and his lovely wife, Eva!

Bruce's twin sister, Vicki, has a sparkle in her eye. She has a wonderful sense of humor, and we marvel at the time she surprised Bruce by showing up at the Bebee Ranch to celebrate their 81st birthday together. I can't think of another time when anyone caught him by surprise like that. She's a beautiful woman, and we love any chance we have to see her. I'm so grateful she gave Bruce the signal that it was safe to come out of the womb.

Bruce H. Bebee and Gail T. Bebee with Gentoo penguins, Antarctica 2025

CHAPTER TWELVE

Time To Make History Again

Bruce is used to adapting to change. There are multiple shifts made due to changes in family, technology, industry cycles, industry moves, and politics, to name a few. Through it all, Bruce maintains the mindset and drive of an entrepreneur.

At age 83, he still genuinely enjoys the challenge of developing unique solutions that few others can, combining mechanical, financial, and mental ability. He describes it as a constantly active brain that sees potential everywhere, from new products to real estate. He views the stress of entrepreneurship as part of the challenge.

Bruce's brain is wired to continually seek design improvements, even in his own equipment. He became frustrated by the rising cost and difficulty of obtaining replacement globes (specialty "light bulbs") for the Night Lights trucks. Their high-intensity output is higher than is really needed for current camera systems. For years, he's been fascinated with LED possibilities, amusing family members by testing flashlights everywhere he found them. Finally, after a nearly ten-year search for more efficient, longer-lasting lighting technology, Bruce was grateful to receive a call from colleague Bill Brennan, who located the LED technology they had been waiting for.

Excited for the possibilities, Bruce and Bill met at night to check the photometrics and test sample lights received from a German manufacturer. Situated outside the Night Lights warehouse at the Bebee Ranch in Texas, they ran through various scenarios to test the LEDs' capabilities.

As the lights pointed to the sky over a quiet Hill Country community, family friend Matt Spannaus noticed an explosion in local social media groups. Locals were suggesting UFO activity, with all kinds of exciting commentary. Matt was familiar with Bruce's business innovations and could tell the light was coming from our general direction, a few miles from his home. He decided to ease the worry by letting the locals know it was his friend testing some lights for his business. Oblivious to the commotion on social media, Bruce and Bill were impressed by the LEDs.

LED test. Bebee Ranch, 2025
Photo Credit Bill Brennan

The test was successful, prompting Bruce to begin building his first LED lighting truck. It will be highly versatile, offering remote control, dimming, strobing, color-changing, and programming. This technological pivot is possible because LEDs have finally reached the required power output for filming. The lights can be controlled one at a time from a cell phone, manually via a lighting board, or via an automated computer program.

The adoption of versatile LED technology will broaden options for filming and open new markets beyond the traditional film, TV, and sports sectors. Bruce anticipates the fun and possibilities for music concerts, festivals, and special events that require dynamic lighting effects. He projects this could increase revenue substantially by enticing new clientele to take advantage of the latest blend of technology and efficiency Night Lights by Bebee is known for. Bruce sees these options as an exciting challenge to make history again through technological innovations and resigns himself to making it happen.

Working side by side as an integral part of the exciting creation of this next-level lighting truck is employee Matthew W. Matthew is a trusted operator, a diesel mechanic, and now a reliable sounding board for new ideas. Hired in 2024, he embodies the ideal employee time and time again. He is a skilled problem-solver who takes initiative and ownership whenever it's called for. Bruce trusts him implicitly to manage operations in his absence, whether it's at the Texas shop, the Georgia shop, the California yard, or on location for a client. Bruce praises Matthew's character and initiative, "He's very loyal, intelligent, and not afraid to get his hands dirty. If one of the trucks has a problem, he jumps right in and takes care of the issue." This "doer" mentality is a reflection of Bruce's own work ethic. Their relationship is a bond of mutual respect and friendship, solidified by regular breakfast meetings and occasional family holiday meals at the Bebee ranch. Though he's been with Night Lights only a short time, Matthew is already welcomed into the "family" atmosphere Bruce cultivates with his key employees.

CHAPTER THIRTEEN

Legacy Is What Others Say

Larry Coulter: Friend and Pastor

It has been said that we discover our life's purpose when we identify our unique strengths and begin to use them. We discover our life's meaning when we use those strengths for the sake of others.

Bruce Bebee has done both.

Growing up, Bruce could easily have been defined by what he lacked—by the abilities he did not have. We all know that experience. As children, we quickly learn to measure ourselves against others and notice who seems to have "more." More musical talent. More athletic ability. More ease in the classroom. Those differences are often painfully visible. For many, that comparison becomes a quiet discouragement they carry for life, shaping their identity around what they lack rather than what they possess.

But Bruce was never held back by what he didn't

have. He refused to be defined by limitations. Instead, he paid attention to what he did have—and then devoted himself fully to developing it. He had a mechanical mind. He could understand how things worked, take them apart, improve them, and make them better. He recognized this gift, leaned into it, and allowed it to shape his life's work. In doing so, he discovered his purpose.

Yet purpose alone is not enough. Purpose without meaning is hollow.

Bruce could have used his gifts in isolation, quietly fixing things and solving problems on his own. Instead, he recognized a need within the entertainment industry and built a company to meet it. More than that, he built people. As he built his business, he invested deeply in the lives of others. He used his mechanical skill not merely to create products, but to cultivate people—helping men discover their own abilities and walking alongside them as they learned to use them well.

In doing so, Bruce transformed purpose into meaning. He gave himself away for the good of others.

That is his legacy.

Donna: Daughter

There are sooooo many years of memories in Las Vegas and at the river house. We enjoyed family time together. The river house was the family gathering place, where my parents, my two brothers, and their families rode jet skis and Sea-Doos. We would take the girls on the Sea-Doos with us since they were so young. We were always taking the kiddos.

In Las Vegas, my husband, Wally, drove the Formula 1 race cars at the Mario Andretti Racing School with dad, my brothers, and uncles. Mom loved the Casinos, but always tried to include the grandkids in things, like trips to Circus Circus. She would also hire babysitters for the grandkids so us kids (me, Wally, Tom, Bruce Jr., and his wife Julie) could do whatever we wanted in the evenings. That meant going to the parties at the Hilton or the Golden Nugget, seeing shows, going out to dinner, or doing whatever we wanted. There are so many good memories.

Tom R.: Son

I was twenty years old when dad sent me out into the field for the 1984 Olympics to hook up generators. Since I went to BIT University, I was fine. BIT University stands for Bebee Institute of Technology. My poor dad had to deal with my curiosity for knowledge. And every time he tried to fix something, I was there looking over, asking him to think out loud. "Teach me, teach me." My mom and dad made such a great team, with dad being so technologically savvy and my mom being so phenomenal on the administrative end.

Las Vegas was a lot of fun. Mom loved to gamble, and she was able to get us tickets to all the shows, boxing matches, and UFC fights. We all went to those, compliments of the Hilton and Golden Nugget hotels. Dad always laughed about going to Vegas because it was one time in his life that he was no longer Mr. Bebee, but "Mitzi's husband, Bruce."

And about the house on the river, there were lots of good times with family playing cards and board games, and taking the kids on my boat. I appreciate working alongside dad on property maintenance, from rebuilding the docks to some construction on the addition.

Patricia Cosulich-Smith: Daughter

When I first met Bruce, I did not understand the significance of the meeting at all. My mom introduced him simply as a friend at the gym, and I gave it little thought. At the time, I did not have a particularly favorable view of men, and even when it became clear they were dating, I kept him at arm's length. Bruce was respectful, patient, and consistent, and he honored my mom's decision to prioritize motherhood before dating.

One day, after a difficult visit with my biological father, I remember hugging Bruce and telling him that I was glad he was going to be my dad. From that point on, that is how I thought of him.

Watching Bruce and my mom build a life together was significant for me. I saw my mother move from being a hardworking, stretched-thin single parent to having a true partner, someone who could match her intelligence, work ethic, and effort. Seeing her happier and more supported mattered to me more than anything else.

As a teenager, I also watched Bruce run a business, and those everyday observations quietly shaped my interest in entrepreneurship. Dinner-table conversations about ingenuity, responsibility, and problem-solving gave me early insight into what business ownership actually looks like, and into the unique challenges and experiences of traditional small businesses. That perspective followed me into college, graduate school, and eventually into social innovation, mentoring founders, and working with entrepreneurs. Bruce helped cultivate that curiosity and interest simply by example.

I consider him my dad in every way that matters, and I often joke that he needs to live to at least 122 so my children, and possibly even their children, can know him too. I have often compared him to the Forrest Gump of mechanics, not because of luck, but because he has repeatedly been present for, and contributed to, moments of real historical and technological significance.

Gary Bebee: Brother

Many people say Bruce is lucky. I'd say his luck amounted to hard work and being willing to take risks. He had the right concept, was always very dedicated and committed to what he was doing. He continues to this day to look towards improving what he's already accomplished. I've always been proud of Bruce and his accomplishments. I'm truly happy for him and the prosperity that came with it. As a handsome young man, he even got the role as an extra in some of the movies with the generator business. Bruce has always remained very kind, thoughtful, and helpful. He's down to earth. It didn't matter if we were playing golf, hunting, in the desert shooting, or one of our many breakfasts or lunches together—he's always a pleasure to be around. When my first wife passed, Bruce was there to help with the aftermath. Likewise, when his wife, Mitzi, passed away, my late wife Phyllis and I extended an open invitation to Bruce for dinner. We've always stayed close.

Brooke: Granddaughter

My step-grandfather, through marriage, has been a monumental figure in my life, profoundly impacting me. He has also been a father figure and an exemplary model for a healthy marriage. Growing up, I was surrounded by toxic and unhealthy relationships, lacking a genuine understanding of what constitutes a healthy partnership. However, in high school, I had the privilege of being taken under his wing and living with him and his wife, Gail, for two years.

These formative years profoundly shaped me and instilled hope that I could achieve a beautiful, healthy relationship akin to the one he has nurtured with his wife. It was incredibly healing to witness a marriage characterized by mutual respect, love, and equality.

Remarkably, during my two years with them, I never once observed them engage in fights or quarrels—a stark contrast to my childhood, when insults hurled at one another were common. Witnessing and participating in such a healthy family dynamic profoundly influenced me and inspired me to strive for a marriage like theirs. Thanks to my grandfather's exemplary influence, I was also able to establish a respectful marriage filled with unconditional love.

Mario: Grandson-in-law

After knowing Bruce for a few years, I finally got the chance to work with him. He was emptying one of his workshops and asked if I could help. I was genuinely excited. Growing up, I had packed up storage units and helped my dad's former company move twice. It was a marketing company, so there were a lot of boxes involved. I went in optimistic and confident, excited for Bruce to finally see my work ethic and endless work tank firsthand.

In my head, I assumed that since Bruce was in his 80s, he would mostly be directing while I did the heavy lifting. My goal was for him to leave to get us food and come back to most of the work already done. Based on my past experiences, I was sure that's how it would go.

That assumption didn't last long.

When I arrived at the shop, Bruce showed me around and gave me a general idea of what needed to be done. There were several huge shelves filled with meticulously organized bolts, screws, tools, and all kinds of parts (very Bruce of him). I immediately spotted a floor dolly and made a plan in my head: take everything off the shelves, keep track of where it all went, lighten them enough to move, roll the shelves on the dolly, and then load everything back on. Simple, fast, and efficient.

Just as I was about to get started, Bruce stopped me and said he had an idea.

I could see his mind working. He asked me to drill holes at the top of each shelf and was oddly specific about the hole size and exactly where each hole should go. At the time, I honestly thought it was unnecessary, but I trusted him and started drilling. He stepped away for a moment to find some nuts and bolts, and by the time he came back—only a few minutes later—his idea was completely formed, and he had everything we needed.

Then he explained the plan.

In just minutes, Bruce had come up with a way to lift the shelves using a forklift. He knew the type of rope we needed, how the pallets should be placed, where everything should sit, and even how the pallets would be loaded. I didn't fully see it yet, so I just kept drilling holes, tightening bolts, and following along.

And then we started moving.

That's when it all made sense. Bruce had figured out how to make tiny, barely noticeable holes that were still strong enough to hold the weight of fully loaded shelves. Somehow, he fit four shelves onto a single pallet with what I could only describe as pyramid-of-Egypt-level precision. I still don't know when, where, or how he measured everything, but it all worked perfectly.

What stood out just as much as the plan was how Bruce worked. He didn't stand back and point—he worked right alongside me. Drilling, lifting, carrying, sweeping, setting up pallets—everything. He moved with a steady, relentless pace, like a man in his 20s.

Other than my dad, I had never seen anyone work with that kind of consistency and determination.

We finished faster than I expected. After that, we moved on to clearing out the office, and once again Bruce immediately had a solution—this time for getting awkward, oddly shaped furniture out of a very small room. By then, I didn't question anything. I just watched, trying to understand how his mind worked.

Bruce has an incredible understanding of mechanics, space, and efficiency. I would move 500 shops with him without hesitation—not just to get the work done, but to learn from him. Seeing his mind at work was rewarding, but seeing his work ethic, his energy, and his willingness to jump in and do the work himself was truly inspiring.

Rochelle: Granddaughter

There were so many special life experiences I had growing up because of my grandpa's generosity and love for his family. His home in Parker was always open to his kids and grandkids. The river will always hold so many childhood memories, like riding jet skis and learning to wakeboard.

Toni Bebee: Sister-in-Law

Bruce has always been the one in our family to get everyone together. He is the instigator of all Bebee family reunions and gatherings. It's been that way for several years, and we truly appreciate it. Without him, I don't think we would all see each other nearly as much. Bruce has been the glue that has held the family together for as long as I have known him (56 years!).

There was a funny incident that my son likes to speak about. He was on leave in the military and figured he would go visit his Uncle Bruce. Bruce teased him about the fact that he had not shaved, "What's this?" To which Michael replied that he was on leave, and Bruce says, "Not when you come to visit me. Go shave that." And you know what Michael says? "When Uncle Bruce tells you to shave, you shave." So he did. I love this simple story because it shows the respect that follows Bruce. People listen to what he has to say.

Vicki and Bruce's 80th Birthday Celebration, hosted by Gail in our Huntington Beach Home. March 2023. Backdrop is a Family tree constructed just in time for the event.
Siblings Left to right: Gary, Vicki, Bruce H. Bebee, Brent

Michael Bebee: Nephew

People often speak about my Uncle Bruce's success, and rightly so. He is a highly accomplished businessman whose professional achievements are easy to admire. When I think about Bruce, however, that is not what stands out most to me. What I admire most is his genuine willingness to be there for others, especially his family. His story is not simply one of building businesses or overcoming obstacles. It is the story of a man who leads with kindness, compassion, and sincere interest in the people around him. Bruce has a way of making others feel seen. He listens. He cares. That authenticity leaves a lasting impression. People do not forget meeting Bruce.

Three Bebee Brothers and Wives at the wedding table of Michael and Felisha Bebee
Front: Brent Bebee, Bruce H. Bebee, Gary Bebee
Back: Toni Bebee, Gail T. Bebee, Eva Bebee
Strawberry Hill, AZ. 2025

Years after Bruce spent time in Las Vegas during the filming of a major box-office movie, I crossed paths with a stuntman who had met him there. Our encounter happened long after that moment, yet the memory remained vivid in this guy's mind. When the stuntman learned my last name, he paused and asked if I was related to Bruce Bebee, the owner of Night Lights by Bebee. He explained that he had met Bruce only once, yet that single interaction had left such an impression that he never forgot the Bebee name. Bruce's warmth, curiosity, and genuine nature stood out in an industry filled with fleeting encounters, and it stayed with him for years. That moment revealed more about my uncle than any list of accomplishments ever could. His legacy is defined not only by what he built, but also by how he made people feel. That, to me, is the truest measure of who Bruce Bebee is.

Gary Kellogg: Brother-in-Law

I met Bruce in 1975. At that time, I was dating his older sister Margo. I remember seeing Bruce's first truck and generator, the beginning of Bebee Generators.

I married his sister, Margo, in 1977 and was welcomed into the Bebee clan. Over the next few years, I watched Bebee Generators grow into the number one generator supplier to the movie, concert, and entertainment industry, and even to NASA for space shuttle landings. All this thanks to Bruce's genius with electricity and knowing what customers needed.

To regress for a moment, you would have had to know Bruce's dad, Clinton. Clint was smart, very talented when it came to anything mechanical. Bruce inherited all that from his dad and doubled it. Bruce has a rare gift: whatever machine he uses, he becomes part of it. I have been with him riding a motorcycle, flying an airplane, driving a truck, and you name it, he always looked like he had done it forever.

Then came the day he sold Bebee Generators, but Bruce could not sit still for long, and Night Lights by Bebee soon became the industry leader in supplying the entertainment business and anyone else who needed special mobile lighting.

In 1996, my late wife Margo was going through very difficult cancer treatments in Phoenix, Arizona. Driving her home 200 miles after that was out of the question.

As always, Bruce stepped up and flew us home in his plane to make the journey easier for her. Unfortunately, Margo passed shortly after, in February 1996. As usual, Bruce and the Bebee family were there to support the kids and me.

Ten years later, I married Kathy. Bruce and his late wife, Mitzi, threw us the greatest wedding reception. You can imagine, again, the Bebee generosity.

But tragedy for Bruce was looming in the future when he lost his wife and life partner, Mitzi. Bruce found love again and married Gail. Night Lights by Bebee remains an industry leader, and Gail makes sure Bruce takes time to enjoy life with many new adventures.

Curt Vogt: Brother-in-Law

I first met Bruce after my sister Gail started dating him. I quickly found him to be a really nice guy and saw a good spark between the two of them. It worked out that they were soon married and building a life together. I got to know him better over time and became increasingly impressed.

As time went on, I learned more about Bruce and the amazing things he had accomplished in his professional life. From the time he started fixing up cars as a young man, to serving his country in the United States Air Force, where he learned the skills that would develop into his own generator business, and then into Night Lights by Bebee, was truly an arc of life I found amazing. Later, when I found out about his reading difficulties, I was even more amazed. It is stunning that he excelled so much despite this and was even considered for the Airmen of the Year at his Base in Alaska. I remember suddenly seeing him read books at a great rate (more like devouring them) when he discovered how to use phonics.

When I was invited to join Gail and Bruce at their

home in the Texas Hill Country, I got to spend more time with Bruce and be around him as he worked on his trucks and lighting systems. His ability to imagine, develop, and build ideas into real, complex working systems is nothing short of phenomenal. Watch him combine designing, mechanical, electrical, and engineering skills to think through and solve problems, and you will see that he just thrives creating like that. It's not just the technical imagination; you'll probably also see him charging forward with those ideas into the workshop to make the things he sees in his head.

You will often find him working diligently as a mechanic, machinist, electrician, welder, or even the guy pushing the broom. Whatever the task is or solution needed, he finds it through learning new skills, hard work, and steady dedication. There is a reason why Bruce has been successful. Plain old hard work. But that is not all. Back to when I first met him… just a real nice guy. He has become more than that. I have seen how he treats other people with kindness and generosity. He easily shares his knowledge with others so they can develop their own skills.

Even better than that, he has become a treasured family member. Thank you, Bruce.

Karalyn Tysdal: Sister-in-Law

The first time that we met Bruce. My sister (Gail) and Bruce drove up to West Hollywood, where we all went to dinner at a barbecue restaurant. Upon taking his first bite of dinner, Bruce started doing a little shimmy dance because he was enjoying it very much. I remember thinking that Bruce must have a good sense of humor and would fit into our family just fine.

Aaron Tysdal: Brother-in-Law

I have heard the nature of an engineer's job is to

solve problems, which I consider a good summary (the point being that facing problems is a good thing; as an engineer, it's part of the job). In hearing Bruce's story of how he developed his lighting trucks, he embodies the qualities of an engineer, a mechanic, and an entrepreneur, seeing a problem on a film set and crafting a solution in his mind.

Patricia D.: Family

Bruce is a very fine, loving husband and father. I remember being at Patricia's college graduation and talking with Bruce. He was so proud of her academic accomplishments and so happy that he was able to support her through college and graduate school. He glowed with pride and happiness for Patricia as a real father to her.

Bruce is always kind and generous with his time. For example, he patiently guided Patricia through her first real estate investment. He thoroughly researched the opportunities, geographic areas, and prospects, and didn't stop until he found the right one (which met all of her criteria), which proved quite profitable!

I admire Bruce for taking the time as an adult to improve his reading skills. He is very disciplined, whether it comes from working out and keeping his body very fit or denying tempting chocolates, except maybe just one a day.

Bruce is open to new ideas, particularly in business, and shares his thinking and encouragement with his wife as a partner. He seems to take life in stride, no matter what is thrown his way; always optimistic and makes the best of all situations with a very calm demeanor. He is a very easy person to go to for help, as he is level-headed and analyzes situations well, especially for others. Bruce is very thoughtful, particularly about others' needs, and helps when he can. In short, Gail, you've got quite a guy there!!! (The author of this book agrees)

Brad Campbell: Friend and Employee

I met Bruce in the early 1990s when he and his son joined my wife and me at my Karate Studio. Right away, he stood out as an extremely hardworking and dedicated student. I would learn later that he approached everything with this mindset. We had over a hundred students at the time, but Bruce and I hit it off right away. He eventually moved, but would still stop by to visit whenever he was in town.

When our studio began to fail, I had no idea what to do. I called Bruce to ask if he might be able to use my help at Night Lights. I knew nothing, absolutely nothing about his business. He told me that if I was willing to push a broom, he would teach me everything. He did just that. He didn't really need me when he hired me, but he took a chance.

Night Lights was an incredible, surreal experience. Bruce's lighting equipment was so respected and sought after in the movie industry. I worked with some of the greatest actors and directors in Hollywood and across the country. When I made a mistake, he made sure I learned from it and then moved on. He never yelled at or belittled anyone who worked for him.

Once I was established at Night Lights, my wife and I finally felt comfortable starting a family. We had been married for fifteen years. We had a son, Ethan, and were able to provide him a stable upbringing, thanks again to Bruce and Night Lights. When it was time for Ethan to go to college, Bruce advised him to major in Business/Finance or at least minor in it because he could use that education in any industry. Our son took Bruce's advice, majored in finance, and is currently working in the finance industry.

Bruce always treated people fairly and was not afraid to give people second chances. Bruce was certainly no pushover. It was not uncommon for him to go head-to-head with the major movie studios over contract issues, usually coming out on top.

To me, he is one of the most accomplished individuals I have ever known. I worked almost thirty years at Night Lights, and I am honored to call him my friend.

Ken Inglett: Friend and Employee

I started working with Bruce as an electrician at Night Lights and eventually became his shop foreman while often operating the lights on location. Bruce has the ability to troubleshoot problems over the phone with his operators. He can also estimate the distance between two points, usually within a half inch or less.

I'm excited to see the new LED truck working and expect the studios will love it. From an operational standpoint, it will be a more efficient use of resources, since the lights will not require the same replacement and maintenance as the globes and fixtures we've used for the past thirty-five years.

Working side by side, Bruce and I quickly became friends, and he became one of my best friends, not just a boss and employee. Our trip to Sturgis and riding our motorcycles around the area was fun and memorable! We rode to Mt. Rushmore and the Eye of the Needle tunnel. I remember seeing Lloyd's baseball hat fly off as he rode in front of me. I was able to hook it on my left foot as I rode. I drove up and gave it to Lloyd, upon which he gave me a crazy, surprised look and exclaimed, “How did you get my hat?!” He did lose his hat again, though. We had a great time!

Bruce Bradford: Friend and Employee

Bruce and I go way back to our teens, when we worked at Arico's, the largest grocery store in Lawndale at the time. Though I have always been close friends with Bruce's brother, Gary, we didn't reconnect until after I retired from my position as Deputy Commander at the Hawthorne Fire Department. It was a chance meeting at the gym. Realizing I was retired, he immediately asked me if I wanted a job, to which I first said, "No, thank you." But then he said, "Let me tell you about it."

Upon hearing about Night Lights and its position in the film industry, I figured it sounded like fun and took the job, promising him I'd stay until I turned seventy. I worked there for several years with many well-known actors. Bruce is brilliant. The lighting trucks he built are simply amazing, far surpassing his competitor's abilities. He quickly dominated the film industry. I particularly enjoyed providing lights for the annual lifeguard competitions in Manhattan Beach, as well as Kevin Costner's "Open Range", filmed in Canada. The people on that one were great, and we all sat together for lunch, including the actors. I am glad I said yes to the opportunity and thankful for the great experience working for Night Lights.

Jim Kiatos: Friend and Employee

Bruce has always impressed me as my Boss, a family man and entrepreneur. Back in 2013, I spent days looking through the classifieds, the old Craigslist, for a very specific Lowrider Harley Davidson motorcycle. Finally, the right ad popped up. I immediately answered and soon found myself at a very impressive facility, with the motorcycle parked outside, all by itself, in a huge, empty lot. I was met by a tall gentleman wearing black polyester pants and a gray T-shirt with the Night Lights Logo. We shook hands, spoke about the motorcycle, and started building a friendship from that moment.

While Bruce and I were talking about the motorcycle sale, the mechanic working in the warehouse at the time, Ed, had opened all the bay doors to reveal a fleet of trucks. I had never seen anything like them before. Their unique design sparked my interest, and I learned that they provide lighting for the movie industry: "We use them for events, production, commercials, and other places that need portable temporary lighting." I was very impressed and asked Bruce if he was looking for any help.

He asked me if I had a Class "A" driver's license. "I do," I responded. "Do you know how to operate a crane?" "I do," I added. "Do you know anything about electricity and generators?" I replied, "I have very little experience when it comes to generators, and I know that electricity can kill you."

He laughed a little bit, and I knew right then and there that I could get along with this gentleman. He gave me a chance to be an operator and trusted me with his equipment. I am still working with him to this day, some thirteen years later. During my time with the "Night Lights by Bebee" organization, I have worked with many other operators and built a great working relationship with most of them, most especially with the owner, Bruce himself.

Bruce is a man of good character. There was a time when I had to make that dreadful call to him regarding damaging a piece of his equipment. I believe it was during the Lucas Oil Off Road Racing Series project at Glen Helen, CA. I was operating the crane and was attempting to wrap the truck for the night after the event was complete. The process is to slowly fold the jib arm alongside the right side of the crane arm. During this process, it is very easy to lose control of this very key step, allowing the jib arm to gain a lot of speed or momentum and slam into the side of the crane arm, which can and most of the time DOES create a lot of damage to the lights, light rack, and other very sensitive pieces of the equipment. I did lose control of this very sensitive key step, and the jib arm did get away from me. It slammed into the side of the crane, causing significant damage to the lights, rack, and equipment. I was very upset with myself and thought I was about to lose my job, one I really enjoy. After some time of stalling, I picked up the phone and made the call to report myself. I'm not used to reporting anyone, let alone myself, to the boss, let alone to the owner of the company. I called, "Hey Bruce, I have some bad news to tell you." He inquired, "OK, what is it?" I answered, "I just broke a light fixture and bent the rack while I was wrapping the truck." "How did that happen?" he asked. "Well, I lost control of the jib while wrapping the truck for the night, exactly what you told me to watch out for and to NOT DO." And after some back-and-forth discussion on how I screwed up, he said to me, "Well, I bet you won't do that again, will ya?" "Bring the truck back to the shop and we will take care of it, don't worry." I was shocked and relieved by how he took the news, and I am still working for the company to this day. I guess Bruce saw the potential in what I was doing and that I would do better in the future. Well, he was correct. I have not destroyed another truck, crane, or light since that day.

I think this little story says a lot about Bruce's character. He is truly a gentleman who understands the efforts that his people put in for him, and he also has their backs.

I have gone to Bruce for life advice before and love what he has to offer. It's much more help than I deserve at times. He speaks to me as if I were a member of his family, not just an employee. I am very grateful. Thank you, Bruce.

Matthew W.: Friend and Employee

Many people go about their lives, adapting to the changes and circumstances that come their way. Bruce, however, changes the world around himself to suit his own ideas. By constantly innovating and upgrading his business, his equipment, and, at times, his staff, Bruce has built the success that surrounds him. Always thinking of the next improvement and following through with trial and, sometimes, a little error. He is great to work with and has taught me a great deal about many things, not just work, in our time together.

Jay Crawford: Friend and Colleague

Bruce and I go way back to the early 80s. I met him when he was working at KTLA in the electrical department. I started talking to him about renting motion picture generators to the studios. We worked together and came up with a design, then he was off on this adventure. In the years to come, I worked with Bruce on some of his concepts with generators and special equipment.

I have always had a great relationship with Bruce for the past forty years. He is the type of guy who always does what he says he will do. He believes it is important to have a good business relationship.

He has been a good personal friend, and I have enjoyed being around him. We had a special time together when we went fishing in Alaska. We brought back enough fish to last my family for a year.

He started his lighting truck company and became a big hit with studios and special events. I used his trucks at my son's high school night football game. This stadium never had any lights, and playing a home game at night was very special to the kids.

I have always had a great relationship with Bruce, and he was always one of my favorite customers, if not THE favorite.

Bill Brennan: Friend and Colleague

Working at Cinema Services in Las Vegas, I was very young and impressionable about all things that produced power and light when my father, James Brennan, introduced me to Bruce. It was 1982, and my father had the only film, television, and theatre lighting company in Las Vegas. This created a lifetime of influence around lighting and generators. Bruce's demeanor was easy-going, and he had a talent for explaining things in a way I could follow. It created a sponge effect on me that I would never lose, absorbing everything I could do with generators and lighting.

My father purchased our first blimped (silent) generators from Bruce for the Caesars Palace prize fights, music videos, and film location remotes in the desert. I was on my way to learning all about power and light from a mentor who would last a lifetime.

As the years went by, Bruce didn't stop dreaming, even after producing some of the finest mobile power plants on the West Coast. It was BIG lighting that was really where he was going. That only increased our relationship in the lighting world. It gave me the unique opportunity to market his technology for lighting BIG events. The Night Lights trucks have accrued an impressive history of events that have impressed the broadcast and film world: Super Bowls, U.S. Swimming Trials, NHL Hockey in Lake Tahoe, Extreme Sports, Film remotes, and anything else that required a lot of light, in places it was never before, and in only minutes.

The Night Lights trucks were a lighting dream that was to become part of my palette, always finding ways and places to light what previously could not be done without them. The Night Lights trucks were my inspiration to see the next possibilities, as the introduction of LED technology began to take hold.

Bruce was sharing future thoughts on utilizing LED technology on a Night Lights truck. This search lasted ten years as we waited for the right product that could perform like an Arc lamp but with LED properties. Last year, a product was finally found. With both of us poised in tacit knowledge and approaching the later years of our lighting relationship, we just might get to see where the next years of lighting BIG events will lead us.

Night Lights by Bebee at 2004 Olympic Swim Team Trials, Long Beach, CA
The historic Queen Mary cruise ship in the background
Photo provided by Brennan Lighting, LLC

Night Lights by Bebee at 2004 Olympic Swim Team Trials, Long Beach, CA
"This was an amazing feat in Lighting history", so says Dick Ebersol of NBC Sports fame.
The Best pool lighting he'd ever seen for broadcasting.
Photo provided by Brennan Lighting, LLC

Nancy L Caruso: Friend

Bruce is an interesting person. He has been around a while and has had many life experiences, which have molded and shaped his interesting life. The thing that stands out to me about Bruce is his high integrity. He means what he says and says what he means. People like that make loyal friends. Friends to the end. Bruce is my friend, and I am lucky to know him.

Tom Caruso: Friend

My friend Bruce is an amazing man. His desire for adventure definitely tops mine, and I thought that was impossible. We have been on vacation together all over the world and still have a few more places to explore—North America, South America, Antarctica, and soon Africa. Although we often take commercial flights together, nothing brought Bruce more joy than being on small planes. Whether it was in a six-seater flying to remote areas in Mexico or a de Havilland Beaver landing on a glacier next to Mount Denali, Bruce loves to fly. I know he has his pilot's license, but I've never had the privilege of being a passenger in a plane while he is the pilot. Even so, Bruce can always be found up front in the co-pilot's chair. He loves to fly.

Bruce is definitely a "trooper" as well. Despite being a few years older than Nancy and me, age never affects him. Our trips are what you call rigorous. In fact, we know from experience that it takes us an extra two days to recover from our own vacations. Bruce is in better shape than anyone I know. He relished hiking in Alaska, trekking through Patagonia, and cruising through the Antarctic Peninsula. He caught a cold in Alaska once and only needed one day off to rest. Who does that? I'm down for two to three days when I get a cold. He's definitely a trooper.

Bruce is a wonderfully adventurous man and a true friend. His integrity is a model for all of us. Thank you, Bruce, for being a special part of our lives.

Bear Watching Expedition, Lake Clark National Park, Alaska, September 2019
Left to right: Patricia Cosulich, Gail T. Bebee, Bruce H. Bebee, Nancy Caruso, Tom Caruso

Jessica Boyle: Friend

My thoughts go back to when my late husband, Larry, would talk about Bruce. Larry said that if he had the chance to pick a close brother-type relationship, it would have been him, without hesitation. From the time Larry originally had his heart failure episode, to the day he passed, he would tell me, "Go to Bruce for anything, anything you need. He will help you and always be your go-to forever." I'll never forget the day that I called Bruce and told him Larry was in the ICU after his first stroke. Bruce and Mitzi picked up our kids in Huntington Beach and brought them to me so they could be with Larry in the hospital up by Magic Mountain. Bruce also picked up Larry's parents from the airport for us. Bruce never stopped being there for Larry as his heart failure episode finally took him from us. Bruce told me back then that he would always be there for the kids and me, no matter what I needed, and I still believe that to be true. He means so much to my family and me. My daughter Dyan recalls her father's relationship with Bruce as a true, loving, do anything for each other type of relationship. I couldn't love him more!!

Ronnie Barnes: High School Friend

What I remember most is that, as long as I have known Bruce, he has always had a smile on his face. I have never heard him say anything bad about anyone. He has always been upbeat whenever we saw each other over the years since high school. But his work ethic and his kindness to others, especially his family, have made him very successful. He paved his way with hard work and long hours. What always impressed me the most was that Bruce always gave credit to those close to him who helped him become successful. And, as always, he would be smiling.

Cathy: Neighbor and Friend

Bruce is truly a special man in so many ways. His intelligence and ingenuity are immediately evident when you first meet him, and he is always willing to lend a hand.

The best example of these attributes was shown when our son was seventeen and completing his Boy Scout Eagle Project. His project was to design and construct storage closets for the Seal Beach Community Center. Due to the Center's class schedule, Curtis had only one weekend to build and paint these large closets. Curtis had coordinated his friends and family to help him and had prepared as much as possible before the construction weekend, but, as always, not everything went according to plan. Bruce was our neighbor and quickly jumped in to offer help. He spent his Saturday down at the Community Center, not only providing his mechanical and construction expertise but also his muscle. He had the tools Curtis needed, and I know he stayed late into the night to help ensure the project would be completed on time.

There are not too many times in our lives when we meet and witness people like Bruce, and I know that I, Karl, Curtis, and Jennifer all feel so privileged to call Bruce our friend. Thank you, Bruce, for being you!

Kitty and Amos: Neighbors and Friends

Bruce was a wonderful neighbor, always ready to help with any repair issue or to lend a hand. He is a good conversationalist and very knowledgeable on many different topics. I am always impressed by how faithful he is about going to the gym and staying in shape. I'm sure having a younger wife is an incentive. It's hard to find neighbors who compared to the Bebees.

Sandra W.: Friend

I'm so happy that Bruce and Gail found each other. 💕 I remember the day they met at the gym and how nervous Gail was! Bruce is a guy who always knows what he wants, and he's not afraid of doing what needs to be done to make it happen - and he knew he wanted Gail in his future!! He didn't just want to get married or have a wife… he wanted to be a husband and a partner, a best friend. It's been fabulous to watch their story unfold. ♥ Bruce has always been in great shape and makes his health a priority, but after meeting Gail and taking a deeper dive into wellness, he became unstoppable! He can outlift guys who are twenty years younger, and his energy level is incredible for a guy in his eighties! He still runs his business, and he and Gail are always on the go. Focusing on cellular wellness gives him a quality of life that most do not have!!

Max M.: Friend

Bruce is someone whose presence naturally makes people feel welcome and at ease. He is charismatic, kind, thoughtful, and genuinely funny—someone who connects easily with people from all walks of life without ever needing the spotlight. What stands out most to me is his creativity as a problem solver and the way he approaches challenges with curiosity, patience, and integrity. He carries a quiet confidence rooted not in ego, but in experience, values, and a deep belief in doing things the right way.

Coming from humble beginnings, Bruce never allowed obstacles—especially his early struggles with reading—to define what he could become. Instead, he leaned into his strengths, worked relentlessly, and continued learning well into later life. The fact that he is now the most avid reader in the family speaks volumes about his resilience and mindset: growth is always possible, and it's never too late to invest in yourself. That lesson alone is deeply inspirational.

On a personal level, Bruce has always been incredibly generous with his time and presence. He has been a true father-figure and friend, always welcoming my brother Guy, our mom Robin, and me into his home—especially during the holidays—creating traditions and memories we will always cherish. Those gatherings reflect who he is at his core: a loving husband, a steady presence, and someone who deeply values family, connection, and showing up for others.

Bruce and Gail also played a huge role in our mother's celebration of life a few years ago, and for that, we are extremely grateful. Their care and thoughtfulness during such a meaningful and difficult time meant more to us than words can express, and it is something we will always hold close.

Above all, Bruce is a kind soul who brings light and joy wherever he goes. He leaves a lasting impression not because of titles or accomplishments alone, but because of the way he treats people—with kindness, respect, and generosity. His life is a powerful reminder that success is built on belief, hard work, integrity, and a lifelong commitment to growth. Bruce truly makes the world a better place simply by being in it.

Ann Sattherwaite: Friend

My main thought about Bruce is how both practical and nurturing he is. He has added and added to his family, being both accepting and supportive along the way. But he doesn't shy away from giving the guidance and advice that is part of being a parent. That's the best parent of all, whether the recipients understand that at the time or not.

Tony and I are honored to consider him a friend.

Jenny Crane: Friend

Bruce Bebee is the embodiment of what it means to age with intention. His energy and vitality reflect someone who refuses to accept decline as normal. He's deeply open-minded about solutions that actually work, always curious and committed to supporting his body at the cellular level. Bruce brings visionary thinking and genius-level ideas to everything he touches, always seeing what's possible before the rest of the world catches up. He also leads the way in aging gracefully, using key tools as part of a daily lifestyle to keep longevity a true priority. Quite simply, the world is a better place because of Bruce; his leadership, innovation, and heart elevate everyone around him.

Adam Woolley: Friend

Bruce is a man whom I've admired greatly since the day we first met. He's innovative, creative, wise, direct, generous, and kind-hearted. He's the kind of guy whom I aspire to be, but still have a lot of work to do.

Colleen and Allen B.: Friends

Bruce's optimistic enthusiasm has impressed us since our first encounters with him. Our respect and admiration have only grown through the years as we see his intentional walk of consistency, discipline, and dedication to a cause! He is a great role model in many regards, including listening and believing in yourself, building solid foundations, and doing it right, with commitment and attention to detail! The care and maintenance for his family, his business, and his personal attention to his work trucks and projects are admirable.

We also admire his outstandingly impressive commitment to his health! In the last eleven years that we've been friends with Bruce, it seems that he has only grown younger and more vibrant! That characteristic, along with his fun sense of humor, adds to the pleasure of being around him, and we look forward to many more years of his company!

Emil Schultz: Friend

I used to work out at 24-Hour Fitness in Huntington Beach, CA. That is where I first noticed Bruce Bebee. He would often be seen doing pull-ups. After completing a set, he would often notice me and others with a nice big smile on his face. We introduced ourselves and commenced discussing situations of interest to each other. I shared that I was an electrical engineer at Southern California Edison. My primary responsibility was doing project development work in the generation project area. Bruce easily understood the work I performed, and we became immediate friends. I learned that Bruce was a successful businessman, highly intelligent, and happily married with a family. Our political views were similar, and we never argued. Bruce and his wife, Gail, hosted annual Christmas parties to which we were invited. My wife, Diane, and I attended and greatly appreciated their hospitality. We hope to remain friends and wish Bruce, Gail, and their family an enjoyable, successful, and happy future.

Stéphanie: Friend

I met Bruce in early 2024. I was genuinely stunned to learn he was in his eighties—he looked decades younger, vibrant, strong, and full of life. At the time, my comparison was my father, who is only a few years older than Bruce but nowhere near as healthy or active. Seeing Bruce standing there, so grounded and energized, made a powerful impression on me. Bruce was living proof of what is possible. He embodies the idea of aging backwards, and I remember thinking, *I want that kind of life—for myself and for the people I love.* Inspired by Bruce's example, I encouraged my father to incorporate what I learned from Gail. Witnessing this change has been deeply meaningful to my family and me.

Bruce is a living testament to the power of intentional living, balance, and commitment to health. I am profoundly grateful for the example he set—not just for me, but for anyone who has the pleasure of meeting him. He continues to inspire others to embrace life to the fullest, showing us what it looks like to live more vibrant lives. Thank you, Bruce!

Laura: Friend

I was lucky to meet Bruce shortly after joining Gail in the pursuit of health and wellness. I can honestly say I did not know his age, nor could I have guessed it, not only because he looked significantly younger but also because he acted like he was. My own father turned eighty a couple of years ago. It was at that point that I discovered Bruce was the same age. The contrast could not be more different. It's all because Bruce puts effort into his diet, lifestyle, and science-based innovations for natural wellness. Amazing to see what life can look like when you prioritize your health. Bruce is the picture of this in spades!

Elle Clavelle: Friend

Bruce is a man with a contagious smile and a heart of gold. He is well accomplished in life, as evidenced by his loving, kindhearted wife. Mr. Bruce is someone you can't mess with about his pull-up routine. In his eighties, he does his pull-ups like Navy SEAL David Goggins. Being present in his life is a blessing, and I will never forget how he makes everyone feel special. I'm grateful to Mr. Bruce.

Mark Browne: Flight Instructor and Friend

Bruce had an amazing passion for flying and an ability to learn so fast, especially for a lack of formal education. It's Elon Musk-like: just different and outside the box, just amazing. He should have designed planes as well as flown them.

Marshal Sylver: Personal Development Educator

Bruce is a remarkable man who has built an amazing life by doing the right things regardless of who was watching. His quick wit and easy style make him the kind of businessman and consultant who massively impacts everything he touches. I am honored to know him and his wife, Gail, and count them among my favorite people on the planet.

CHAPTER FOURTEEN

Enduring Impact

Legacy is most clearly measured not by what is accumulated, but by what is sustained—across generations, across hardship, and across lives quietly changed. Bruce exemplifies a life defined by enduring commitments: two lasting marriages that model devotion, respect, and resilience; a family that grew from four children to include eight grandchildren and eight great-grandchildren; and a professional journey marked by history-making achievements through the creation of two industry-leading companies. Rooted in humble beginnings, Bruce speaks gratitude, "The odds of (me) getting here were low. But it just takes drive and determination. It's been a good life."

Bruce engineered and built the first and largest soundproof generator company in Hollywood, serving multiple industries, the U.S. government, and major sporting events. Proving to himself that he could succeed again, he did the same by building one of only two large mobile lighting companies in the U.S. Having accomplished this and assessing next steps at age 83, Bruce chuckles, "One of my children is retired, one is getting ready to retire, and I'm still working. Logically, it's time to relax, do just a few jobs…but it's time to make history again." He is thriving on the creation of a breakthrough in next-generation mobile lighting.

Bebee Generators and Night Lights by Bebee were both hands-on family enterprises that integrated Bruce and Mitzi's kids into technical and operational roles, shaping their careers and family trajectories. They were encouraged and mentored to learn by doing. Their roles fit their strengths, and responsibilities were added as they gained confidence and demonstrated dependability. Bruce speaks of this generational legacy with pride, noting that his kids accomplished their own success in the industry that provided them with the security and opportunity as a family. "I do have to say, all four of our kids have grown up to be successful and decent humans. There is a lot to be said about that. They gave us beautiful grandchildren, who in turn gave us very beautiful great-grandchildren. Life is good."

Beyond family and enterprise lies a deeper inheritance—an unwavering record of kindness, loyalty, and generosity that is often quietly carried out. Whether opening doors to those in need of a place to live; offering bridge loans at critical moments; paying employees through industry shutdowns; gifting personal growth seminars to family and employees; mentoring others to start their own business; or helping children purchase their first homes, his legacy is built on leading by example, modeling self-sufficiency, mentoring others, and showing up when it matters most. His story is a testament to a life lived with purpose, integrity, compassion, and an enduring belief that success means lifting others as you go.

As with most successful entrepreneurs and mentors, Bruce's lived experience provides perspective and wisdom. This is one of the things that endeared him to me early in our relationship. We share similar outlooks on so many things. The following are direct quotes I've recorded from Bruce, alongside my version addressing the same subject matter. It should be easy to see why we get along so well. While we are aware that not everyone will see the world the same way we do as a couple, it is a blessing to be with a spouse who is on the same page. Bruce is not only a man with fine-tuned mechanical skills, but also one of integrity in all that he does. His logical mindset and calm demeanor are only topped by his love of family and friends, who may or may not understand the wisdom behind his leadership. And that's okay.

On personal responsibility: "No matter your circumstances of what happened to you or for you as a child, eventually we all must take personal responsibility for the choices we make as adults." Avoid the trap of victim mentality and seek help if you feel stuck in this paralyzing mindset.

On work ethic: "Do what needs to be done—even if that means you are cleaning the bathroom or pushing a broom." No one is above any job. Be a team player, whether you are the boss or the employee. It will open up possibilities you can't even imagine.

On education and personal growth: "Never stop learning. Go to college or a tech school. Invest in personal growth. Learn to read, or whatever will help you move forward." When we stop learning, we stop growing, and we are in a state of decay. As a point of validation, Bruce and I attended two personal growth seminars together within the last six months. Thank you for the invitation, Michael and Felisha Bebee. Bruce enjoyed it immensely. I especially enjoyed watching him and mentor Marshall Sylver run calculations and possibilities in their heads while helping our cohorts brainstorm ideas to help scale their businesses. It was through this series of seminars that I committed to writing this book. Thank you, Marshall.

On finances: "Going into debt to develop a product or to achieve growth toward higher return makes sense, as long as you are willing to invest the time and effort it takes to succeed. But going into debt for the purpose of having expensive toys or vacations can get you into trouble. When you carry heavy debt, you may not recover in a downturn. Have at least 6 months to a year of operating expenses on hand so that if things get slow, you have options. If you have debt, make sure it's controllable." Just because you can qualify for a loan does not mean it's smart to do so. I was told early in my oil and gas career to strive to save at least a year, if not two, of living expenses. Every job I've ever had was in a cyclical industry. I'm grateful for that early advice and grateful Bruce is financially prudent.

On choosing a life partner: "A man is unlimited in what he can accomplish with a strong, independent woman supporting him. Together as partners, they can do just about anything." Likewise, a man who is supportive of a woman, whether in business or in family matters, is a keeper! I'm grateful that Bruce supports my business endeavors in health and wellness, even as we lovingly refer to him as my "walking billboard." He's also been immensely patient throughout the creation of this book, written almost entirely as we've traveled across the Southwestern United States in an RV. I lovingly joke that I have him "captive" long enough to record his stories and transcribe them for you, because at home, he always has a project. His response to this is, "I've never had a woman want me to keep talking so long." Thank you, Bruce. I love your humor and your heart.

The conversations we've had as I've been writing this book are endearing, and I cherish them.

On employees: "Surround yourself with disciplined, reliable people; skills can be taught when the foundation of character is strong." Good character is often overlooked, but it is truly one of the most important traits of co-workers, colleagues, friends, and family.

On growing a company: "No, one person creates a company, and no one person keeps a company alive. It takes a good team of drivers and support personnel who represent the company well. Granted, I'm the one who designs it and is responsible for troubleshooting if they can't handle something. It's up to me to make sure the trucks are maintained. Without a good team, it would probably be a one- or two-truck company, and I would have to work night and day. Success is limited by the number of quality people you have behind you. I will also say you need a good spouse who understands what you're doing and is willing to take the financial risk." Surround yourself with people who represent the company respectfully. Personal language, appearance, and attitude are every bit as important as technical ability and having safe respect for the equipment. The most valuable employee is often the one who can fill any role with competence and a positive attitude. Everyone is important.

On ego: "Don't be afraid to hire someone smarter than you and don't be afraid to ask for help." You cannot be an expert in everything. You will limit your life experience and influence if you always consider yourself to be the smartest or most important person in the room.

On income diversity: "If you have a business, you have to understand: you have expenses, and it doesn't matter whether you have a dime coming in or not. Those expenses keep going, and it's up to you to cover the cost. For a year and a half with no work, it was up to me to keep the company afloat, and I was able to. That's the whole advantage of having set yourself up with more than one income stream. Create multiple sources of income, or as you've heard many times, diversify, so that one earthquake won't destroy everything you own." Yes!

On loaning money: "I'm always pleased when they pay me back. Usually they do". It's not always so much about the money as it is about embracing personal responsibility. When we come to terms with that mindset, it makes all the difference in our future.

On handling stress: "I guess you would say that stress is part of the driving challenge for almost any entrepreneur. Find a healthy release, whether it's reading, singing, working out, pulling weeds, or going for long walks." If you find yourself constantly angry or turning to substances, understand that this will likely become your ultimate unravelling and seek help.

On parenting: "It takes a lot of patience and a good sense of humor. It helps to know who you are." I've heard this said by parents of multiple generations, likely because it's pretty accurate. If you are a parent, you may be nodding your head, yes? Our pastor once commented in his sermon that all families are complicated. He invited anyone in the congregation who had not yet experienced this to let him know, and he was happy to introduce us to his family. Love and grace conquer all, not only when given, but also when received.

In short, I provide you with the following summary for those who may have jumped to the end when deciding whether or not you can glean success tips by reading this entire story of entrepreneur, Bruce Harper Bebee: "Believe in yourself. Fine-tune your skills. Identify potential needs in the market. Identify the level of risk you are willing to take. Play to your strengths. Work Smart. Be diligent. Surround yourself with positive, growth-minded people. Be open to advice. Prepare for possible bumps in the road. Accept personal responsibility. Give and accept grace. Enjoy life and adjust all of the above when necessary."

Good advice. Amen. Good night.

About the Author

Gail T. Bebee believes her prayers were answered when she met her husband, Bruce Harper Bebee, though it took her a moment to realize it. Raised in Boulder, Colorado, she earned a degree in Geophysical Engineering from the Colorado School of Mines and started her career in oil and gas exploration before retiring as an Engineering Geologist. As a single working mother, she was deeply involved in church, Scouting, and her daughter's school. A family health crisis sparked her passion for health, wellness, and anti-aging science, shaping her current work in natural wellness. Grateful for God's creations and family, Gail now happily shares life with Bruce in the Texas Hill Country.

Take a closer look at the work through which Bruce sets industry standards at https://www.nightlightsbybebee.com

www.ingramcontent.com/pod-product-compliance
Lightning Source LLC
LaVergne TN
LVHW010916110826
845149LV00013B/2377

* 9 7 8 1 9 6 0 6 6 5 3 2 4 *